Real life, real answers.

How to buy your first home

How to buy your first home

by
Peter Jones

Houghton Mifflin Company   Boston
1990

For information about permission to reproduce selections from this book, write to Permissions, Houghton Mifflin Company, 2 Park Street, Boston, Massachusetts 02108.

Library of Congress Catalog Card Number: 89-85922
ISBN: 0-395-51100-3

General editors: Barbara Binswanger, James Charlton, Lee Simmons

Design by Hudson Studio

"Real life, real answers" is a trademark of the John Hancock Mutual Life Insurance Company.

Printed in the United States of America

10 9 8 7 6 5 4 3 2 1

Although this book is designed to provide accurate and authoritative information in regard to the subject matter covered, neither the author and general editors nor the publisher are engaged in rendering legal, accounting, or other professional service. If legal advice or other expert assistance is required, the services of a competent professional should be sought.

Contents

Introduction

Y ou're thinking about buying your first home. You aren't sure you have enough for a down payment. You're concerned about qualifying for a mortgage. You're afraid you won't be able to find a house you'll like at a price you can afford. In fact, you are worried about the whole unsettling, unfamiliar process. After all, this will probably be the single most important financial decision of your life.

This book will help you every step of the way. Despite all the headlines about the skyrocketing costs of home ownership, the odds are good that you'll be able to buy a house. Nearly half of America's 25 to 34 year olds today own their own homes, an encouraging statistic considering all the financial obstacles they have had to overcome.

THE FIRST-TIME BUYER HURDLE

Since 1970, the median price of a new, single-family home has increased by more than 400 percent, from $23,400 to over $104,000 in 1989. As for existing homes, the median price climbed from $23,000 to $85,000. Prices in different areas of the country vary tremendously, of course. The median price of a house in San Francisco was about $235,000 in 1989. In Louisville it was less than $60,000. Keep in mind that "median" means "in the middle"; half of all houses were priced below these median numbers.

Nevertheless, most first-time buyers must come up with from $10,000 to $20,000 or more in cash as a down payment on a house. To do that, some turn to their families. Others find government-financed programs that help. Many go on tight budgets, save every possible dollar, and raid every source of lump-sum money they have, from company profit sharing plans to the new car that can be traded in for a clunker plus cash.

It *is* harder to buy a first home today than it was a generation ago. The cruel truth is that the cost of housing has far outpaced the cost of living in the past 20 years. There are bills pending in Congress that could help, and many states are also considering new ways to make first-time home ownership easier. However, those bills may not apply to you. And who knows whether new legislation will be passed in time to help you.

Later on in this book, you'll find a few ideas that may help right now. With some sacrifices, hard work, and a little ingenuity, you *can* become a home owner.

IS OWNING A HOUSE STILL A GOOD IDEA?

After years in which many home owners saw the value of their houses increase in double-digit percentages annually, houses have recently appreciated at a far slower rate, or not at all, in many areas of the country. In a few areas, property values have actually declined. Some people believe that single-family houses are no longer the "sure thing" they once were in terms of investment potential.

There's a chance they're right, of course. But there are no other sure things in sight either. Historically, housing prices over the long run have risen at a rate that at least parallels, and usually surpasses, the rate of inflation. Even during the Depression of the 1930's, housing prices declined only 39 percent while the stock market fell as much as 89 percent. In the more recent recessions of 1974–1975 and 1981–1982, housing prices managed to rise an average of 10 percent.

Owning your own home is still a sound, long-term investment. Maybe the first house you buy won't appreciate in value the way it might have in the 1970's and 1980's, but you will be building equity in it to use when you buy a second house—which also won't have appreciated as much.

Appreciation isn't the only financial reason for investing in a house instead of renting. The federal government has always encouraged home ownership, and the latest tax laws left the private home as one of the last viable tax shelters for the average American family. If you own a home, you can still take a number of deductions that lower your income tax bills. And when you sell it, you'll pay no taxes on your profit if you buy a house of equal or greater value. When you are 55 or over, you get another tax break—a one-time exclusion from taxation on up to $125,000 of profit realized on the sale.

RENTING

Before you commit yourself to buying a house, take a good, long look at your reasons for doing it. Certainly there are some circumstances in which renting is preferable, including the following.

- ☐ If you are going to move out of the area within three years or so, you are probably better off renting. You incur substantial closing and borrowing costs when you buy any house and, unless the house appreciates very quickly, you could end up losing money when you sell it.

- ☐ If you live in an area where rents are low and houses are not appreciating or are even depreciating in value, you might be better off renting and putting your down payment money in some other investment. On the other hand, the best time to buy a house may be in a bad real estate market; you are likely to find a bargain that will look even better in a few years when the market recovers.

- ☐ If you hate the very idea of becoming a part-time plumber, gardener, carpenter, and painter—and know you won't be able to afford the parade of professionals offering those services— renting is a better idea than the misery of home ownership. Owning a home is a lifestyle decision as well as an investment decision.

Also remember, when renting, the majority of your investment money is not tied up in a single property, and you aren't restricted by anything other than a lease if you decide you want to move.

On the other hand, if you continue to rent, you will have less privacy, no tax-saving deductions, and no hedge against inflation.

MORE REASONS TO OWN

If you live in someone else's building, you have a pile of rent receipts at the end of the year that aren't worth a thing. With a similar pile of mortgage payment receipts, you have a record of growing equity in your home and a way to ease the pain of federal and state taxes. Consider these owner benefits:

Interest deductions

When you first start paying off your mortgage, only a small percentage of your monthly payment is applied to reduce the principal amount owed. Most of what you pay will be interest charges, and they are 100 percent tax deductible.

Property taxes

These are fully deductible. If your interest payments plus your property taxes are $10,000 a year and you are in the 28 percent tax bracket, owning a house has saved you $2,800 in federal taxes you would otherwise have paid.

Home loan deductions

The 1986 tax laws phased out virtually all of the deductions once allowed on interest payments. Aside from mortgages, the only loans on which interest can still be deducted are home improvement loans, refinanced mortgages, and home equity loans.

A home office

If you can prove that you work at home and you meet the IRS

requirements, you can legitimately deduct a percentage of your home-operating costs equal to the amount of space your office occupies. If you have a seven-room house and use one room exclusively as an office, you can write off one-seventh of your gas, oil, electric, mortgage interest, property taxes, insurance, and maintenance and repair expenses. Be aware that the rules have gotten a lot stricter in the past few years. If you are thinking of a home office in your new house, talk to your tax adviser beforehand.

If you plan on operating a business out of your home, rather than just establishing a home office, check the local zoning laws before you buy to ensure that you can do so legally.

Tax advantages, building equity, and the opportunity to make a profit on a house when you sell it are hardly the only reasons to own a home. Most people find it emotionally satisfying. They like knowing they can decorate and remodel as they please and entertain people whenever they wish. They like the privacy the home ensures. They enjoy the security of raising a family in a place that is theirs.

STEP-BY-STEP TO OWNING YOUR FIRST HOME

If you want to become a first-time home owner, you will go through most or all of the steps listed below. There's no exact timetable. Depending on your financial situation, you could be weeks or years away from moving in. It could take days or months to find the house you want. But however long it takes, you will do the following in roughly the order suggested, the same order in which the rest of this book is organized to help you:

1. Decide how much you can afford in terms of both down payment and monthly carrying charges.
2. Decide how much you want to spend (it may be less than you can afford).
3. Choose areas and neighborhoods you like and can afford.
4. Decide on the kind of house you want to live in: an older house

5

or a newly built one, single-family or two-family, condominium or townhouse, split-level or contemporary, small plot or large.

5. If you are on a very tight budget, as most first-time buyers are, set priorities about the features you want in a home while being ready to compromise on the less important features.

6. Read real estate ads and develop a good sense of prices and local market conditions.

7. Find and work with a good real estate agent.

8. Inspect enough houses so that you can make intelligent comparisons that will help you make a final decision.

9. Make an offer to purchase, and then negotiate terms.

10. Hire a real estate lawyer.

11. Sign a contract to buy.

12. Have the house inspected.

13. Apply for and receive a mortgage loan.

14. Attend the closing and complete the purchase of your first home.

CHAPTER I

What can you afford?

B uying a first home is a decision that will affect your social life, leisure time, commuting patterns, the education of your children, and practically every other aspect of your life. But the financial aspects are your primary concern at the moment. Even if owning a house is a form of saving in the long run, today's prices and mortgage rates are pushing first-time buyers to levels of spending that can easily threaten their financial security.

What can you afford? One of the traditional guidelines used by many home buyers was to multiply gross annual income by two and a half; that figure was the maximum amount that should be paid for a house. If you made $30,000 a year, you could afford a house that cost $75,000.

High debt loads, high mortgage rates, and sharply increasing property taxes have made that multiplier less useful. Probably the best way to figure out what you can afford is to start with the standards applied by mortgage lenders; first, because it's in their interest to lend money to people who will be able to pay it back; second, because if you use their rules now, you will reduce the risks of being turned down for a mortgage later.

THE 28 PERCENT RULE

Most lenders now prefer to focus not so much on the total price of the house, but on how the buyer will manage to carry the monthly costs of owning it. Therefore, they allow a family to devote up to 28 percent of its income to cover the costs of principal and interest payments on the mortgage, property taxes, and homeowners insurance. But they will also take into account any other long-term debt you have, such as a car loan, a time payment for a major appliance, a college tuition loan you are still repaying, or revolving credit card debt. Your total monthly debt payments, including housing, should not exceed 33 percent (some lenders will go as high as 36 percent) of your gross monthly income.

Keep in mind that the standards lenders use to decide how much you can afford aren't necessarily the same criteria you want to apply. The lender isn't concerned about how difficult or unpleasant it will be for you to live with your debt load. The lender only cares that you are a good credit risk and that you are likely to repay the loan on schedule. So after you go through the qualifying tests in this chapter, you must decide whether or not you want to devote as much of your income to housing as the lender is willing to allow you.

YOUR OTHER DEBTS

Before you apply for a mortgage, you should examine your other debts and, where possible, reduce or eliminate them. You aren't "saving money" if you do not pay off credit card balances but instead put the money in the bank. In fact, given the interest rates those cards charge, you are losing ground fast.

Lenders know this. That's why they will make you account for your other long-term debt on your mortgage application forms. Here is a short version of a questionnaire a lender might use:

	Total owed	Monthly payment
Automobile loan	$_____	$_____
Other installment loans	$_____	$_____

Margin accounts	$_____	$_____
Credit card balances over 60 days	$_____	$_____
Other debts	$_____	$_____
Totals	$_____	$_____

Your total monthly payments on debt should amount to a maximum of 5 percent (8 percent for some lenders) of your gross monthly income. The questionnaire that follows will help you establish that. If your percentage is higher, try to reduce it before you apply for a mortgage.

FINDING THE DOWN PAYMENT

The catch-22 of home ownership is that when you own a house and want to buy another one, you will have ready access to the down payment for it. You'll be living in it. But right now, buying a first home, you may be hard pressed to find an adequate lump sum of money.

How much will you need? If it is at all possible, you should try to make a down payment of 20 percent of the total price of the house. The minimum down payment with a conventional mortgage loan is 5 percent. You might also qualify for an FHA (Federal Housing Administration) or VA (Veterans Administration) backed loan, which requires an even smaller or possibly no down payment. But the smaller the down payment, the higher other costs will be.

How much can you scrape together for a down payment? Start by listing your assets in the questionnaire that follows and deciding which ones can be turned into cash. Just because life insurance policies and Individual Retirement Accounts (IRAs) are listed does not mean that you should cash them in. Remember, a house is a priority, but it isn't the only one you have.

Don't be too proud to ask for help from your families. It is best if they give you an outright gift, not a loan. A loan will be added to your other long-term debt by the lender when he considers your mortgage application. Because the federal gift tax regulations allow anyone to make a tax-free gift of up to $10,000 to another person in any calendar year, your parents can give you and your spouse up to $40,000 ($10,000 from each of them to each of you), and nobody has to pay taxes on it.

If your family is able to help, get the money a few months beforehand and invest it in CDs or money market funds. That way, when you talk to a lender, those assets will be seen as yours. Some lenders don't like the idea of an entire down payment coming from the buyer's family. Others may require a "gift letter" from your family or parents. A gift letter states all the terms of the gift, including the fact that it does not have to be repaid.

Don't lose heart if you fill out the questionnaire and it is obvious you have nowhere near enough cash for a down payment. Try getting creative. The love of Jack Stetson's life was the 1965 sports car he had bought and painstakingly restored in his bachelor days. But when he and his wife decided they wanted to own a house, the car turned out to be their best source of ready cash.

You need to know what your assets are so that you can figure out how much you need to raise. Then you can develop a reasonable plan to do that. That plan might be as simple as a stringent savings program. Other ways to find the money for a down payment are discussed in Chapter III.

A MORTGAGE BORROWER'S FINANCIAL QUESTIONNAIRE

Lenders have a long list of questions that they want answered before they approve a mortgage loan. They want to know in detail your current assets and liabilities as well as your monthly income and expenses. In fact, the following questionnaire may be somewhat less exhaustive than some lenders require.

Your earnings

The lender not only wants to know how much money you make, but where it comes from.

Base salary	$_____
Overtime	_____
Commissions	_____
Bonus	_____
Dividends and interest	_____
Child support	_____
Alimony	_____
Pensions	_____
Nontaxable income	_____
Other income	_____
Total annual income	$ _____

Note: Both members of a two-income family should fill out the above form, then add the totals to reach a combined total annual income.

Average monthly expenses for nonhousing items

Food and household supplies	$ _____
Clothing	_____
Medical, including insurance premiums	_____
Insurance	_____
Automobiles	_____
Education	_____
Travel (commuting)	_____
Recreation	_____
Interest charges on credit cards	_____
Installment payments	_____
Child support	_____
Alimony	_____

Telephone	
Dues, fees	
Personal expenses	
Savings and investments	
Taxes	
Total monthly expenses	$ _____

How much can you spend on a down payment?

This question is essentially answered by determining your current total assets. If you have any liabilities other than the long-term debt total you recorded a couple of pages back, deduct that amount to reach your net worth.

Cash	$ _____
Bank and money market accounts	
CDs and other savings	
Stocks and bonds	
Mutual funds	
Life insurance policies	
Vested pension funds	
IRAs	
Other	
Total worth	$ _____

QUALIFYING FOR A FIRST HOME

The worksheet on pages 16 and 17 will tell you what you want to know: the estimated maximum purchase price of your first house. When you have that estimated number, the next step is a prequalifying interview with at least one potential lender. Ask a real estate agent to set up an appointment for you with one or two of the financial institutions that service the area where you intend to buy.

Such an interview won't commit you to anything when you actually begin to shop for a mortgage in earnest, but it will help you adjust the numbers in the worksheet to local conditions. As a first-time buyer, you want all the input and information you can get.

Using the information from the questionnaire on pages 11 and 12, fill in the worksheet on pages 16 and 17.

MORTGAGE RATES

Chapter V will help you decide what kind of mortgage is best for you, where to find it, what to look for in a good one, and what to look out for. But no matter what kind of mortgage you get, there will be two variables that greatly affect how much the loan will cost you: the rate of interest and the number of years involved.

Interest rates continually rise and fall depending on market forces beyond your or your lender's control. The lower interest rates are, the more you can afford to borrow on your mortgage. If you have an $80,000, 30-year fixed-rate mortgage at 10 percent, your monthly payments will be $702.40. The same mortgage at 12 percent raises the monthly payment to $823.20. The 2 percent difference translates into a whopping difference of $43,488 in payments over 30 years.

How much will that $80,000 cost over 30 years? Much more than the face amount. Here are the numbers:

$80,000 Mortgage for 30 Years at 12 percent

Monthly payments	$823.20	
Total number of payments	360	(30 years x 12 months)
360 x $823.20 =	$296,352	in total payments
Minus principal	$80,000	
	$216,352	total interest

At 10 percent, the total interest payments would be only $172,864. Now see what happens when you change the other variable: time.

$80,000 Mortgage for 20 Years at 12 percent

Monthly payments	$881.60	
Total number of payments	240	(20 years x 12 months)
240 x $881.60 =	$211,584	in total payments
Minus principal	$80,000	
	$131,584	total interest

A difference of just $58.40 in monthly payments for 20 years ($14,016) saves $84,768 in interest.

Balancing off your desire to pay the least amount of interest for the shortest period of time against your need for a low monthly payment is a critically important long-term decision. But you must also look at the other factor that will affect the size of your monthly payment.

MAKING A HIGH DOWN PAYMENT

The higher your down payment, the lower your mortgage. The lower your mortgage, the lower your monthly payment. With a lower mortgage, you have a greater opportunity to shorten the term and save on interest payments.

That's easy enough, but only if you have the money in hand. No matter how hard it is going to be to raise that money, you should be aware of the case for the highest down payment possible. A large down payment:

☐ Gives you immediate equity in your home.
☐ Reduces your monthly payments.
☐ Helps you get better terms on your mortgage.
☐ Eliminates the need to buy mortgage insurance.
☐ Saves on long-term interest payments.

Lenders insist that you have a personal stake in the property you are buying. That protects them against a downturn in the market. Some people who had made low down payments in the Houston area in the early 1980's simply walked away from their houses, allowing the banks to foreclose when the real estate market declined sharply.

MONTHLY PAYMENTS PER $1,000 OF MORTGAGE LOAN

Interest Rate %	10 Years	15 Years	20 Years	25 Years	30 Years
8 1/2	12.40	9.84	8.68	8.06	7.69
8 3/4	12.54	9.99	8.84	8.23	7.87
9	12.67	10.14	9.00	8.40	8.05
9 1/4	12.81	10.29	9.16	8.57	8.23
9 1/2	12.94	10.44	9.33	8.74	8.41
9 3/4	13.08	10.59	9.49	8.92	8.60
10	13.22	10.75	9.66	9.09	8.78
10 1/4	13.36	10.90	9.82	9.27	8.97
10 1/2	13.50	11.06	9.99	9.45	9.15
10 3/4	13.64	11.21	10.16	9.63	9.34
11	13.78	11.37	10.33	9.81	9.53
11 1/4	13.92	11.53	10.50	9.99	9.72
11 1/2	14.06	11.69	10.67	10.17	9.91
11 3/4	14.21	11.85	10.84	10.35	10.10
12	14.35	12.01	11.02	10.54	10.29
12 1/4	14.50	12.16	11.19	10.72	10.48
12 1/2	14.64	12.33	11.37	10.91	10.68
12 3/4	14.79	12.49	11.54	11.10	10.87
13	14.94	12.66	11.72	11.28	11.07

To compute a monthly payment, select the prevailing interest rate from the left-hand column. Then read across to the column headed by the term (number of years) of the loan. Multiply the number indicated by the number of thousands of dollars of the mortgage loan. Example: suppose you have an $80,000 mortgage loan for 25 years at a fixed rate of 9%. Read down the Interest Rate % column until you find 9%. Then read across the 9% row to the 25-year column. You will see the number 8.40. Multiply 8.40 by 80. The result is $672, which is the amount paid to the lender of the $80,000 loan each month for principal and interest payments only. Your actual monthly payments will be $672 plus one-twelfth of your annual property taxes and one-twelfth of your annual home insurance premium.

ESTIMATED MAXIMUM PURCHASE PRICE

1. CASH AVAILABLE FOR A DOWN PAYMENT

Available cash	$ _____
Sale of assets (CDs, stocks, bonds, etc.)	_____
Cash gifts	_____
Total cash to be raised	$ _____
Less closing costs (estimate 5 percent of the amount of your mortgage)	_____
Total cash for down payment	$ _____

2. GROSS MONTHLY INCOME

Combined annual income	$ _____
	Divided by 12 months
Gross monthly income of all persons listed on the mortgage loan	$ _____

3. AFFORDABLE MONTHLY PITI

Generally, lenders allow you to allocate up to 28 percent
of your annual income to payments, interest, taxes,
and insurance (PITI).

(a) Gross monthly income (from part 2)	$ _____
Percent of income for PITI	x .28
Affordable monthly PITI	$ _____

Lenders will allow about one-third of your gross income
to be allocated to paying off debts such as your mortgage,
credit cards, car loans, installment loans, etc. Some will go
as high as 36 percent, the percentage used here.

16

(b) Gross monthly income (from part 2) $ _____

Percent of income for debts   x .36

Affordable monthly PITI with debts $ _____

Minus actual debt payments other than
for housing   _____

Affordable monthly PITI $ _____

(c) Enter the smaller PITI (a or b) $ _____

4. AFFORDABLE MONTHLY PRINCIPAL AND INTEREST (PI)

Affordable monthly PITI (from part 3 section C) $ _____

Minus estimated taxes and insurance   _____

**Affordable monthly payment for
principal and interest payments (PI)** $ _____

5. MAXIMUM AMOUNT OF MORTGAGE LOAN

Use the amortization table on page 15 to estimate the
maximum loan for which you can qualify, based on current
interest rates for a fixed rate mortgage. It should be
no larger than PI in part 4.

Enter the maximum amount $ _____

6. MAXIMUM PURCHASE PRICE

Enter down payment from part 1 $ _____

Add maximum mortgage loan from part 5 $ _____

Estimated maximum purchase price $ _____

A twenty percent down payment will satisfy most lenders on a conventional loan. It's a good number to shoot for, even though the minimum required for a conventional loan is 5 percent (it can be less or even zero if you qualify for an FHA-insured or VA-guaranteed loan). A lot of other costs will increase sharply when you put down less; these will be discussed later.

MAKING A LOW DOWN PAYMENT

There are two sides to just about everything, and down payments on a house are no exception. There are some positives about a low down payment, which should come as good news if you don't have any choice in the matter anyway.

Taxes

Uncle Sam loves home owners, and the higher your mortgage interest payments, the more you will save on taxes.

Appreciation potential

This is a dangerous game to play, but if housing prices escalate rapidly and you sell the house within a few years, you will have used "leverage" to turn a tidy profit. Example: you buy a $100,000 house with a down payment of $10,000. Five years later you sell it for $200,000. On an initial investment of $10,000 you've turned a thousand percent profit. If you had put down $20,000, your profit would be "only" 500 percent.

Liquidity

The lower your down payment, the easier it may be to find cash for emergencies and the inevitable costs of moving into and furnishing a home.

WHAT CAN YOU AFFORD?

You should have a much better idea now than you did at the beginning of this chapter. But don't be too concerned about making final decisions just yet. As long as you have a fairly good idea of your maximum price, you're ready to start looking.

Real life, real answers.

Jim Kaufman, a sales representative for a national automotive parts distributor, and his wife Beth, a freelance graphic designer, got married five years ago when they were both 27. Their first child is now two, and Beth is six months pregnant. For three years, they have been living in a two-bedroom garden apartment in a suburb 12 miles outside of Chicago and have been saving money for a down payment on a house.

The Kaufmans' gross annual income is $43,000. They've got $9,000 in a money market fund, $8,000 in a stock mutual fund, and $6,000 in an IRA, which they don't want to touch unless absolutely necessary. They've figured out that they can afford $1,000 a month in PITI; this was confirmed by a local savings and loan association. With a 20 percent down payment, they know they can get a fixed-rate mortgage at 10 percent.

After two discouraging months of house hunting in the area in which they now live, and in which they would like to remain, they've had to face the fact that the lowest price for the three-bedroom, two-bath house they would like is in the $150,000 range. But this week, they saw a "handyman's special"—a house owned by a couple in their eighties who hadn't done any remodeling or much maintenance for at least 20 years. It has only one ancient bathroom, but it is structurally sound and in a neighborhood of houses worth at least $30,000 more than the asking price—$110,000.

The Kaufmans' agent is sure they can get the house for $108,000, so they work out a monthly PITI, based on a down payment of $22,000:

Monthly payments on $86,000	
30-year, fixed-rate mortgage @ 10%	$755
Taxes @ $2,800 a year	233
Insurance @ $300 a year	25
Total monthly PITI	$1,013

Tight, but close enough. Beth's parents don't like the idea of the Kaufmans' cleaning out their IRA, and have offered to give them up to $7,000. With $3,500 in closing costs and a lot of remodeling to be done, the Kaufmans are nervous. But if their first bid of $102,000 is accepted . . .

CHAPTER II

What to buy and where

You're going to make a lot of decisions before you find the right house. The first one, having established the maximum price you can afford to pay, is whether or not you *want* to pay that much.

There's certainly no rule that says you must stretch your resources to the limit and buy the most expensive house possible. If a couple of years without a get-away-from-it-all vacation sounds too grim to bear, face up to it now. If you are very conservative about money, you might be more comfortable buying a smaller house or condominium and putting the rest of your money in some other investments. If you anticipate incurring other heavy expenses in the near future, such as taking care of an aging parent or sending your children to college, you have to decide what your priorities are.

On the other hand, many people treat their first house as their primary investment instrument. If you have no unusual expenses and are reasonably certain your income will increase over the next few years, you should probably consider buying the most house, in the most desirable area, that you can afford. That may mean a few years of carrying a house that consumes practically every extra dollar you earn. But if the raises come on schedule, each year the expenses of the house will become less of a burden. And by the time you are ready to trade up, you may have achieved some healthy gains that will more than repay you for those first lean years.

LOCATION

The oldest saying in real estate is that the three most important factors in buying property are location, location, and location. Put a handsome mansion on a lot adjoining a garbage dump, and it might be worth less than a tenth of what the exact same house on the exact same lot would bring if it were in the best neighborhood in town.

Obvious, right? But there are far more subtle examples of the location factor at work. Put exactly the same house on exactly equivalent lots in exactly equivalent neighborhoods in two adjoining towns. Why would one house be priced $50,000 more than the other?

That's the kind of question you will wrestle with when you choose a town and a neighborhood in which to buy your first house. It could be that property taxes are lower in one town. If you have a choice between paying $3,000 or $4,000 in taxes each year and everything else is equal, you'd be willing to pay more for the house with the lower tax rate.

Perhaps the schools in one town have a better reputation. Or garbage gets collected three times a week in one town, but you have to cart it to a dump yourself in another. Use the neighborhood checklist on page 24 to rate the availability and quality of basic services and amenities in the different areas you are considering.

Shopping neighborhoods

The emphasis on location also means finding an area that is compatible with your lifestyle. Here's a brief checklist of some of the questions you should ask yourself. The idea is simply to get you started doing some hard thinking about what is important to you, your spouse, and your family. So don't stop with the questions here; ask a lot of your own.

Yes	No	
☐	☐	Are you willing to commute 30 minutes? Sixty minutes? Two hours?
☐	☐	Do you want to live close to your place of work because you need access at nights and on weekends?
☐	☐	Do you feel a need to "get away" from work to an entirely different environment?
☐	☐	Do you prefer total privacy?
☐	☐	Do you like having close neighbors?
☐	☐	Is public transportation important?
☐	☐	Is it important that your home be near a school? A hospital? A shopping mall? Public or private recreational facilities?

Whether you decide to live in a city, a suburb, or the country, you will want to establish just what kind of neighborhood you are considering. Drive or walk around. Are you comfortable just being there? Do you like the way people maintain their homes? Where do the children play? How do people dress?

Try to meet some people. It's easy to strike up a conversation in a supermarket; most people will be glad to talk to someone who is thinking about moving into their neighborhood. If you have friends in the area, ask if they can introduce you to some of their neighbors. Talk to people, listen to them, and decide if you are going to be comfortable being part of their community.

When you begin house hunting, you are going to spend a good deal of time with the classified real estate ads in the local papers. But don't stop there. Read the rest of the paper as well. Get a sense of local community issues surrounding schools, taxes, crime, and the environment.

Talk to some local business people: bankers, insurance agents, local store owners. Ask about taxes, how stable an area they think it is, what they think it will be like in the future. Get a sense of zoning regulations, any major new construction planned, and other prospective changes; a visit to town hall might be fruitful.

Some people spend weeks shopping for the right car and

only an hour or two investigating where they want to live. Don't be one of them. This is the most important shopping expedition of your life.

Remember: it's an investment

One final reminder about the importance of location. Maybe you really wouldn't mind living next to a garbage dump, and the house next to it looks like an attractive bargain. Just keep in mind that someday you are going to want to sell your house. Will it be difficult to find a buyer? If the garbage dump keeps getting larger and larger, will the house depreciate in value?

Most of us aren't going to consider houses next to garbage dumps. But the principle is sound. Two tips:

☐ Don't buy the most expensive house in the neighborhood. It's always harder to resell such a house. If you can find a modest house you like in a neighborhood of more expensive homes, it has better potential for appreciation.

☐ Don't buy a house in a neighborhood that is going through a downward transition. Prices may be lower than for comparable houses elsewhere, but they may be headed lower yet. Ideally, you will do the opposite: buy a house in a new neighborhood that will become more attractive with the passage of time or an older neighborhood that is undergoing a revival.

OLD VERSUS NEW

While you are deciding on one or two areas you think you might want to live in, you should also be considering whether you want to buy a new house or an old one. And, new or old, do you want a single-family house or a condominium? Perhaps you should think about a two-family house that can provide you with an income as well as shelter and appreciation potential.

What you ultimately settle on will be a matter of personal choice, although, depending on the area, new construction may simply be out of your price range. In any case, there are pluses and minuses to both old and new homes.

NEIGHBORHOOD CHECKLIST

Use this checklist to find the neighborhood with the services and amenities most important to you. You can either make notes on each one or come up with your own system of 1 to 10 ratings.

Community Services and Facilities

Police department
Fire department
Hospitals
Post office
Municipal water supply
Municipal sewers
Garbage collection
Utilities (gas/electric)
Cable television
Library
Churches
Public transportation
Shopping facilities
   Supermarkets
   Pharmacies
   Department stores
   Hardware store
   Garages
   Other
Restaurants
Recreational facilities

Schools and Children's Activities

Public schools
   Elementary
   Secondary
Private schools
Parochial schools
Special schools
School transportation
"Y" and other community centers
Little League
Playgrounds/sports facilities

Potential Problems

Too much traffic or noise
Rising property taxes
Factories/industry
Pollution
High crime rate
Too many vacant buildings
Decrease in population
Too few families with children
Home prices decreasing

The good side of buying new

A newly constructed home, particularly if it is not completely built at the time you agree to buy it, offers several advantages:

Customization. Builders are often willing to customize to some degree to accommodate your personal preferences—on the grade of flooring, for instance, or perhaps the type of bathroom fixtures. But changing floor plans or anything else can get expensive; find out exactly what each change will cost.

Financing. Builders will often offer you financing through their own lenders at a lower percentage than the current rates on other mortgages.

Latest construction standards. Presumably, a new house has been built to meet all of the latest building code rules and regulations. It will have good insulation, for instance, which will mean lower heating and air-conditioning bills.

Appreciation potential. If you choose the right development and area, new houses can appreciate faster in the first few years than houses in older, more established areas. New homes also tend to be built with the requirements of today's move-up market in mind.

The down side of new construction

Delivery schedules. When you buy a house under construction, it is wise to add at least a couple of months to the completion schedule promised by the builder. Make sure the builder is reputable. There are horror stories galore about builders going bankrupt and leaving dozens of families not only without homes but without their down payments.

Evaluating the neighborhood. It can be hard to tell what the neighborhood will be like if you are one of the early buyers in a new development.

Shoddy construction. There are countless ways for a builder to shave costs and keep building inspectors from catching poor workmanship or inferior materials. People have been known to move into a brand-new home and have it literally fall apart.

Concrete crumbles in the basement. Improperly kilned framing lumber twists as it dries inside walls, causing the sheet rock nailed to it to bulge and crack.

In some states, you can buy a new home warranty that will pay for any builder-oriented problem that arises in the first five or ten years after the house is built. But that represents an additional cost that adds between $3 and $5 per $1,000 of the house's sale price. In a few states, builders must carry warranty insurance, but you can be sure that the cost of it is passed on to buyers.

Higher taxes. More often than not, new housing is taxed at the highest current going rates. After all, new players always have to pay to get in the game.

High cost of landscaping. You'll be surprised at how much a few bushes and a tree or two can cost. And how long it takes for landscaping to look established.

A new-home buyer's checklist

If you do decide on buying a newly built home, here's a quick checklist of what to look for and things to do:

Builder reputation. Check with the local Better Business Bureau for any complaints against the builder. Ask your lender to do a credit check on him; the last thing you want is to deal with someone who is in poor financial condition. Talk to people who have bought houses previously built by his company. If the builder is reputable, he'll be glad to supply you with names. Don't expect any builder to be beloved by his past customers; you are looking for serious complaints.

Warranties. Try not to buy a newly built house without one. A good warranty will guarantee the house against major structural defects for up to 10 years, and any problems caused by poor materials or workmanship for the first two years.

Hire your own architect or independent building inspector. This is not absolutely necessary if you feel confident in your own ability to judge the builder's work, but it can save a lot of money and grief in the long run. Either way, you should conduct periodic inspections of the house as it is being built. This right should be written into the sale agreement with the builder.

The "punch list." A few weeks before your final settlement date, you and the builder (accompanied by your architect or inspector and perhaps your lawyer) should conduct a major inspection of the house together to make up a "punch list" of defects that must be corrected and of work still incomplete. The list should be as exhaustive as possible and be signed by you and your builder. By signing the punch list, he is agreeing to correct all of the problems you have identified before settlement.

Settlement. As a practical matter, even if all of the items on your punch list haven't been taken care of by settlement, you may not be able to refuse to settle if you don't have another place to live. Let your attorney handle negotiations with your builder. At best, part of your settlement money will be put into an escrow account that the builder won't get until he corrects the defects. If the defects are minor, you may agree to pay him in full, but get his written agreement that the work will be completed within a specified period of time.

The final chapter on closings and settlements covers more details that are applicable to buyers of both newly built and old houses.

The best part of old houses

There are advantages to old houses, too.

Sturdy construction. Construction materials have improved over the last couple of decades, but, except at the upper price levels of new construction, craftsmanship has not.

Established neighborhoods. What you see is what you get.

Low-cost landscaping. A well-established lawn and landscaping mean not only fewer bills but a lot less time spent on tiresome chores.

Complaints about old houses

Higher down payments. Resale homes tend to require larger

cash down payments, since you are not dealing with a builder who can afford financing at a reduced rate.

Older appliances and fixtures. The appliances in an older home may not be state of the art and will need to be replaced sooner than those in a new home. Older sinks and toilets do not have the benefits of improved function and design.

Systems need upgrading. Older homes often need major work done on electrical, plumbing, and heating systems. This can be expensive for you but not financially rewarding in terms of increasing the house's resale value. Older houses often have insufficient insulation, too, and insulating the exterior walls of many older houses is a gory and expensive process.

Early inspections

No matter what shape the house is in, you should have a professional inspection done after you reach an agreement to buy it—with the purchase dependent on certain aspects of the inspection. But if you are thinking of buying an old house that is obviously in need of major repairs, perhaps even structural work, you don't have to wait. How else will you be able to estimate what repairs and remodeling will cost? Simply tell the owner you want to have the house inspected before you make a bid. If he or she won't allow it, walk away.

You can get a list of members of the American Society of Home Inspectors by calling (202) 842-3096. An inspection followed by a written report will cost from $200 to $500 for most homes in most areas.

TYPES OF HOUSES

Especially for first-time buyers, the type of house you will buy will depend to a large degree on what is available in the area where you want to live. There may not be any newly built single-family homes at all, or perhaps the only homes in your price range are condominiums. Nevertheless, it's a good idea to review the main types of houses available.

Condominiums

These are single-family houses that are either attached to the houses on either side of them, stand alone, or are apartments in a multilevel building. They are purchased rather than leased on a monthly basis. What makes all of them condominiums is that you buy the rights to your apartment or unit outright and also own a share in the common areas of the development along with the other condo owners.

Common areas can include everything from swimming pools and golf courses to hallways and landscaping. The advantages of condo ownership include such amenities along with all the tax benefits of single-home ownership. In addition to your monthly mortgage payment, you'll pay a monthly maintenance fee to maintain common areas, but you'll never have to use a lawn mower yourself.

Condominiums are often the choice of first-time buyers who don't need the space of a larger home (although condos can be very large indeed), prefer not worrying about maintenance (particularly important when both spouses are working full-time), and want all of the tax benefits and appreciation potential that owning a house provides.

Townhouses

These are legally a different form of ownership than condominium ownership. You individually own the land on which a townhouse sits as well as the structure itself, although there may be common walls with other owners. In common usage, townhouses are usually attached row houses.

You'll find block after block of old townhouses in major cities, especially in the Northeast. You'll also find new townhouse complexes that have the same kind of amenities offered by some condominium complexes. One of the advantages of townhouse ownership is that it is usually somewhat easier to get financing than with a condominium.

Real life, real answers.

Joe Demerest, 34, drives a delivery truck in Hart-ford, Connecticut, for an air express service. His wife Susan, 30, works part-time in an adult care community and takes care of their two children, aged six and two. Their combined income is $34,000.

Living in one of the highest-priced housing areas in the country, the Demerests have been renting a two-bedroom unit in a two-family house. They've dreamed about a house of their own but didn't think they would ever be able to afford one. Now Joe's father, a widower, is selling his house in Hartford and retiring to a small condominium apartment he has bought in Florida with an old friend. His father has offered to give his son and daughter-in-law a $20,000 gift from the proceeds of his house. Added to the $12,000 in savings they have, the Demerests suddenly find themselves with enough for a down payment.

Their problem now is carrying costs. Their 28 percent PITI works out to less than $10,000—enough to cover a mortgage in their high-tax area of no more than $70,000. So the Demerests decide to look at two-family houses and come up with these numbers:

Price of two-family house	$150,000
Minus down payment of 20%.	30,000
Mortgage needed	$120,000
Monthly carrying costs for 30-year $120,000 adjustable-rate mortgage @ 8.5% *	$923
Monthly rental of second unit in house	$700 *
Mortgage payments minus rental income received	$223
Plus taxes (real estate and on rental income) and insurance	$450
Monthly PITI	$673

The riskiest part of owning a two-family house is the possibility of not being able to rent for a period of time. Fortunately for the Demerests, a cousin of Susan's has agreed to a two-year lease at the $700 monthly rental. The Demerests know how much work the owners of a two-family house must do, but they feel that's a small price to pay for a dream come true.

---

* The Demerests are counting on rents from the second unit in the house to keep up with increased costs if the interest rate on their mortgage goes up.

Single-family houses

The vast majority of individually owned homes in America are single-family, unattached dwellings that invariably fit into one of seven basic architectural designs: colonial, ranch, split-level, bi-level, Cape Cod, Victorian, or contemporary. There are no financial advantages or disadvantages to any of the designs. People buy one type or another strictly as a matter of personal taste and according to what happens to be popular (and therefore easily resalable) in their area.

Two-family houses

A two-family house may have been built as two complete units that are one or two stories high and separated by a thick party wall, or as a two-story building that has two entrances, one for the upstairs and one for the ground floor unit. Larger single-family houses can often be divided into two complete sets of living quarters, each with a bath, kitchen, and other rooms.

When you own a two-family house, the rental you get on the second unit can go a long way toward meeting your own monthly PITI and house maintenance costs. Especially if you are willing to take on some plumbing, electrical, and other chores yourself, you may find owning a two-family house an attractive first-time option. In fact, some two-family house owners are able to cover all of their monthly costs with their rental income, living virtually free in their own unit while the entire house appreciates.

Before you rush out to bank your rental income, though, be aware of the possible complications. First, check to see if there are any restrictions on rentals in the area. The existing tenant may be paying $150 a month and rent stabilization laws may prevent you from raising that to what you think is a fair market price. Second, allow for the possibility of periods when you will earn no rental income. Tenants do move, and finding a new one to move in immediately may not be easy. Finally, while two-family houses generally appreciate in value at the same rate as other houses, they often don't sell as quickly. Keep that in mind if you think you might need to sell on short notice.

THE IDEAL HOUSE

Everybody dreams of an ideal house, but few of us ever get to live in one. And first-time buyers are the least likely to find anything that comes close to the ideal home they hope can someday be theirs.

Being realistic about what you really need, as well as what you can afford, is essential when you are shopping for a first house. You are going to have to make a lot of compromises. You're probably going to have to settle for less house than you would like in a less desirable area.

Now's the time to face up to reality and make some hard choices. You've already investigated neighborhoods and have found areas that are affordable and meet your needs. Take a few minutes now to decide your minimum requirements about space, and your own priorities about important features.

As you fill out the "What Do You Really Need?" checklist, keep in mind you are trying to establish *minimum* standards acceptable to you. If you find a house that beats some of them, wonderful.

WHAT TO LOOK FOR

Looking for a house, deciding how much to offer for a house you like, making an offer, negotiating, and going to contract are all part of a process that is best covered all at once. You'll find that in Chapter IV. In the meanwhile, look over the "House Buyer's Checklist" on pages 34 to 35. No matter what its design, there are basic requirements that any house has to meet. No first house will be perfect, of course, but you have already set some of your own priorities and should remember them as you look at the questions on the checklist. Later, use the checklist with each house you seriously consider, modifying it to fit your own individual needs and preferences.

WHAT DO YOU REALLY NEED?

This checklist will help you to decide what is most important to you, what you might like but can live without, and what you don't care about at all.

Rooms

Living room. How big is your present living room? What is the minimum size your new living room should be? Think in terms of furniture.

Family room. Do you really need one? If you do, does it affect how big your living room must be? Do you want a fireplace?

Bedrooms. How many do you need? What's the minimum size of the master bedroom?

Bathrooms. Do you need more than one? Will one bathroom and a half bath be enough?

Kitchen. How large is your current kitchen? Do you want more counter space? Drawers? Cabinets? Do you have to have a dishwasher? How large must the eating area of the kitchen be?

Dining room. Do you want a formal dining room? If it isn't important, what kind of eating areas will be needed in either the kitchen or the family room?

Closets. Think about all of your storage needs.

Basement. Do you need one? A finished basement? Storage space?

Other. Do you need/want any separate areas for special interests and activities? A home office? A game room? A workshop?

Exterior/Garage

Garage. Do you need one at all? One car? Two car? Attached? Is storage space necessary?

Deck/Patio/Porch. Which do you prefer?

Yard. Do you want a large yard? Small? Space for a garden? Enclosed for pets or small children?

List the rooms and minimum sizes you prefer	List the rooms and sizes you'll settle for
Living room _____	Living room _____
Bedrooms _____	Bedrooms _____
Bathrooms _____	Bathrooms _____
Kitchen _____	Kitchen _____
Family room _____	Family room _____
Dining room _____	Dining room _____
Garage _____	Garage _____

HOUSE BUYER'S CHECKLIST

Exterior—General

☐ Are the surfaces of the driveway and sidewalk in good condition, or will they need resurfacing?

☐ Does the drainage system carry water off the roof and at least four feet away from the foundation?

☐ Are there outdoor lights at all of the doors?

☐ Are the gas, electric, and water meters on the outside of the house? If not, can they be moved outside?

☐ Is there storage space for the lawn mower and gardening tools?

Interior—General

☐ Are the bedrooms separate from the living areas so that people can sleep while other activities are going on in the house?

☐ Are the bedrooms large enough for the persons who will use them?

☐ Will the furniture you own or intend to buy go with the house?

Storage

☐ Is there a closet near the front door?

☐ Are there enough adequately sized closets in the bedrooms?

☐ Are there enough storage areas in other rooms of the house?

☐ If there is a shortage of storage areas, are there areas that can be converted to storage?

Kitchen

☐ Is the kitchen adjacent to the dining room or other eating area?

☐ Is the work triangle formed by the storage, cleanup, and cooking areas convenient?

☐ Is there enough counter space?

☐ Is there enough storage space?

☐ Will the appliances need to be replaced?

☐ Is there space for a washer and dryer near the kitchen (or bedroom)?

Baths

- ☐ Are there enough baths for your family?
- ☐ Are all the bathrooms conveniently located, and are they large enough?
- ☐ Are there stains or chips in the bathroom and/or kitchen fixtures?
- ☐ After the toilets flush, do the tanks fill with water and then shut off without dripping water or hissing air?
- ☐ Do the drains in the sinks and basins empty quickly and completely?

Support Systems

- ☐ Is the heating and cooling equipment in good running order?
- ☐ Is there adequate insulation in the walls and attic?
- ☐ Is there a service contract for the furnace and air conditioner?
- ☐ Do the thermostats work properly?
- ☐ Is the electrical service enough for the house? Electricity should be at least 100-amp service with 220–240 volt circuits for clothes dryers, ovens, and water heaters.
- ☐ Are there enough outlets in each room? Current electrical standards call for an outlet every seven to ten feet along all walls of every room. Kitchens should have at least two separate circuits feeding into them so that you can run your coffee pot and the toaster at the same time and not blow a fuse.
- ☐ Is the hot water heater in good working order? When will it need to be replaced?
- ☐ Is water pressure at the taps good? The water in a house should gush out of every tap.
- ☐ Is the house connected to municipal water and sewage systems, or is there a septic tank?
- ☐ Does the septic tank need draining, or will a new one be needed?
- ☐ If there is a water supply well, is it working?

CHAPTER III

Strategies for first-time buyers

T he discussion of down payments in Chapter I may have left you feeling a bit lost. *Wasn't this book supposed to help me every step of the way?*

Unfortunately, it's doubtful that anyone else is going to save money for you, and putting down *some* money of your own is nearly essential and certainly preferable. Remember that approximately one-third of all first-time home buyers get some form of financial aid from their families. Ideally, that is in the form of an outright gift. But if that's impossible, look into a loan.

FAMILY LOANS

Taking money from a relative is filled with emotional complexities on both sides. Can your parents or relatives provide you with the money you need and leave you alone in terms of how to spend it? How will you feel if you have trouble paying a loan back? Do you really want to risk money your relatives have saved for retirement?

If you do borrow money from relatives, make sure that the agreement itself is a sound legal document. You can buy legal forms for loans at most stationery stores. Specify as many details as possible on the form. Pay a reasonable rate of interest; you might choose a percentage somewhere between what the borrower would earn if the money were placed in a safe investment such as a CD and what you would have to pay if you were able to get a bank loan.

Think of a loan from a family member as no different than one from a bank. The real stress point in family loans occurs when the payment schedule isn't met. One way to ease the dangers of a family war is to state in the loan agreement that any unpaid debts will be treated as money owed the relative's or parent's estate and will be deducted from the borrower's inheritance.

There are two last-ditch possibilities you might consider if the down payment still eludes you and you don't qualify for an FHA-insured or VA-guaranteed loan (see below).

Shared equity

If your parents or other relatives need tax deductions, look into sharing equity in the house with them. In such an arrangement, they might put down most of the down payment in return for half ownership of the house. As co-owners, you would each pay part of the mortgage, insurance, and real estate taxes; you would each deduct your share from your income taxes.

Shared equity is complicated, and you'll need a lawyer to work out the details, including who is responsible for maintaining the house, what happens if one co-owner wants to sell and the other doesn't, and how to resolve disputes.

Co-signing a mortgage

If you don't yet have an established credit record or the lender just won't give you a mortgage on your own, it is possible to have a relative or friend co-sign the mortgage with you. He or she won't be responsible for the payments (that's your check to write), but if for any reason you default on your payments the co-signer becomes totally liable for repayment of the loan. Obviously, this isn't an obligation either of you should take lightly.

HELP FROM THE FHA AND VA

The Federal Housing Administration (FHA) and the Veterans Administration (VA) either insure or guarantee certain mortgage loans that have very low, and sometimes no (in the case of a VA loan), down payment requirements. There are upper limits on the amount of an FHA loan that vary in different parts of the country, but anyone can now qualify for one. You must be a veteran to qualify for a VA loan (see Chapter V, on finding a mortgage, for more information).

BUYING STRATEGIES

Your grandparents and perhaps even your parents might have bought one house that they lived in happily ever after. The economics of residential housing today make that unlikely in your case. What matters today is to get into a house that you can use to build up your equity. You've already thought about your minimum needs. Following are some strategies to consider.

Rent with an option to buy

Suppose you have just changed jobs and are making a lot more money than you did just two months ago. Many lenders might be hesitant to give you a mortgage until you have worked at your current salary level for a while longer. You may be able to rent a house with an option to buy at an agreed-upon price within a year. Typically, in such an agreement, some or all of your rent payments would be applied to the purchase price of the house.

This tactic is popular when mortgage money is hard to get or the rates are particularly high, since it may be the only way the owner can get rid of his property. But it is also an excellent way for you to live in a house, see if you like it and the area, and save money for a down payment in the meanwhile.

Look for an improving neighborhood

Find a neighborhood that has been depressed but is just beginning to turn around. City dwellers do this all the time.

Choose an area that is run-down but shows signs of gentrification. Buy a house that needs some work, fix it, and sell it as the neighborhood becomes more fashionable. Professional renovators who do this for a living have some guidelines:

- [ ] Slums usually *don't* turn around.
- [ ] Most restoration work occurs in working-class neighborhoods that are on the fringe of the center city and/or adjacent to the real slums.
- [ ] Look for an area where some, but not too much, restoration work is already going on. Timing is everything for maximum appreciation, and by the time it is obvious to everyone that a neighborhood has turned around, it will be too late for a bargain.
- [ ] Locate the pocket of existing restoration in the area and then pick a house within a five-block radius. The cost of the house should still be low, but the chances of other restorers filling in the gap are excellent.

Build a kit home

If you are reasonably adept with tools, and if you can find the time on weekends, during vacations, and at night after work, you can buy land and build a kit home purchased from one of dozens of U.S. manufacturers. Most manufacturers offer services that range from architectural consulting and tailoring a home to your needs to sending advisers to your building site and even recommending contractors to do part of the work for you.

Your work will have to pass local building inspections, and you could end up working long hours for several months. But you will also spend a lot less money than if you bought a house already built; typically, when a kit house is finished, it will be worth twice what you paid for it.

Generally, you cannot buy a kit home unless you already own the land free and clear. And you cannot get a mortgage on a house that doesn't exist. But if you have all the building permits needed, you should be able to get an interim construction loan that can be converted into a mortgage once the house is completed. The kit company will require a down payment with your order—usually at least 25 percent—with the balance due on delivery.

Take on a handyman special

Sometimes the best buys are the houses nobody wants to touch. Not many people have the imagination to walk through a run-down house and see its potential. For example, many old houses have enormous kitchens—enough space for two or more rooms if you can see past the broken stove, rusted refrigerator, and worn-out linoleum.

A lot of first-time buyers with no prior experience at building anything have taken on such houses, put in a lot of sweat equity, and ended up with a both a sense of accomplishment and a house that has greatly appreciated in value.

A house inspection—done by a paid professional, not a relative who "really knows a lot about houses"—is an absolute necessity. If any major structural problems are detected, such as a crumbling foundation or load-bearing walls that are rotting out, you may want to rethink your purchase. Defects like these mean you'll have to hire a contractor, and that expense might erase any potential margin of profit.

Check out foreclosures and auctions

When people fall on hard times and can't pay their monthly mortgage bills, their homes revert to lenders who put the houses on the market, often at bargain prices. Someone else's misfortune can suddenly become your good luck.

Foreclosed houses are always being sold, and sometimes auctioned, by the federal agencies and private companies that insure or buy mortgages. You can get a schedule of both foreclosures and auctions by calling a local bank or savings and loan association. In most cases, you'll be given a list of properties and/or referred to the local real estate agencies that are marketing the houses for the lending institutions.

Real life, real answers.

Beth and George Tate were looking for a house in an expensive suburban area. For months they exhausted the patience of first one and then another real estate agent. Most of the starter houses, at least the ones they wanted to start with, were $250,000 to $400,000, but Beth and George had $140,000 as their limit. Then, one Wednesday, the real estate agent they had been working with for the past few months called to say there was a house for $125,000 that he thought would be sold by the weekend. It was in a great location overlooking a river, had four bedrooms, two baths, and many of the amenities the Tates had seen only in more expensive houses. The drawback was that, despite its charm, the building needed major repair work.

Forewarned, the Tates took an inspector along the next day. They were able to buy the house for $115,000, putting down $24,000 in cash. For the next eight months they devoted their weekends and all of their vacation time to the house. They shored up the foundation at one end of the basement, painted every room, redid both bathrooms, refinished the floors, and did a lot of cosmetic repairs. They never got to the aging roof and ignored the rewiring that needed to be done as badly as the walls needed insulation.

Their out-of-pocket costs were $25,000, much of it borrowed from their parents. In less than a year they put the house on the market again and sold it for $225,000. After settling their mortgage and paying back their parents (with interest), they had $109,000. About half of that became the down payment on their second house—one that the Tates made sure needed no work at all to make it livable.

In the case of federal agencies, both the U.S. Department of Housing and Urban Development (HUD) and the Federal National Mortgage Corporation (Fannie Mae) advertise properties in the real estate sections of newspapers and sell them through local housing offices or real estate agencies. Fannie

Real life, real answers.

For 15 years, Bill and Betty Adams lived rent-free in a house provided by the private school in Maine where Bill taught chemistry. Betty worked part-time as a tutor while raising their two children. That added about $4,000 a year to Bill's salary of $24,000.

Then Bill took a job with a major industrial company in California, 3,000 miles away. It paid $50,000 a year—more than twice his teaching salary—but the Adamses would now have to pay for housing.

After a whirlwind weekend of house hunting, they found a house they liked and could afford. The problem came when they applied for a mortgage. Bill was just starting his new job. The loan they wanted was based on his new salary level, but he hadn't been working at that level long enough to qualify for a mortgage.

Luckily for the Adamses, when they explained the situation to the seller, he agreed to rent them the house for a year with an option to buy at an agreed-upon price. Best of all, he agreed that, since the Adamses would pay all costs of maintenance, repairs, and utilities, 100 percent of the rent could be applied to the purchase price.

Twelve months later, after being introduced to a local bank by Bill's employer and establishing an account there, the Adamses were able to get a good mortgage and buy the home they had been living in for a year.

Mae also has a toll-free number (800-553-4636) that handles requests for information.

Don't assume a foreclosed house is necessarily a bargain. It could be in need of extensive repairs. It may have legal claims against it that a new owner would have to settle. If the original owner is still living in it, six months might pass before you could legally force him or her to leave.

A house can be put up for auction to settle an estate, because of a foreclosure, or because of a bankruptcy of a corporation, a builder, or an individual home owner. Auctions are always announced in local newspapers well ahead of the auction date, so you can inspect the property before bidding on it. When you buy a property at auction, you will be expected to present a certified check for a stipulated amount, such as $1,000, to show good faith while you make the necessary mortgage loan arrangements.

Be subsidized

Many local governments, particularly those of larger cities, offer subsidy programs to help people buy houses. Some of these programs are funded by local bond issues; others get their support from state and federal agencies. Some programs subsidize the purchase of homes at mortgage rates several points below market rates. Others defer local property taxes for long periods of time.

Still other programs are virtually homestead acts that give people a variety of incentives to move into dilapidated houses in poor areas, fix them up, and live in them for a minimum period of time, such as five years.

Check your state and local housing departments to see what programs are available and if you qualify for any of them. At the same time, check with the nearest office of the U.S. Department of Housing and Urban Development (HUD). It's possible there is a loan program available for the area you are considering.

If you want to buy in a rural community, can't obtain a mortgage elsewhere, and otherwise qualify (there are income ceilings and other guidelines that must be met, but you *don't* have to be a farmer), you may be eligible for a Farmer's Home Administration (FmHA) mortgage loan. Check a local office of the FmHA or write the Farmer's Home Administration Office, U.S. Department of Agriculture (Washington, DC 20250).

Buy off-season and in bad times

Traditionally, most people go house hunting in the spring, so demand along with prices are then at their peak. The next busiest time is fall. But when the ground is covered with snow, or it is stifling hot, or it is raining all the time, people who are selling houses usually don't see many potential buyers. When one shows up, they may be in a mood to negotiate.

The weather and seasons affect the market to some degree, but there's nothing like a recession or skyrocketing mortgage rates to put a glut of houses on the market. Builders who got caught with half-built houses are eager to make deals. Sellers who absolutely must sell will make lease-option deals, take back mortgages, and reduce prices.

Look for a good deal when not many others are looking at all. The odds are you'll find one.

Go farther away

The closer you live to an urban center, the higher your housing costs. Is more house for a lot less money worth a one- or even two-hour commute twice a day?

Share a house

A lending institution considers two, three, or four incomes better than one. Some married couples are even joining forces and buying a home they can share. Two or more single people are doing the same thing. Mortgage lenders have been a little slow to respond to such untraditional lifestyles, but most now realize that the loans they make may be even more secure with several people responsible for repayment.

If you are planning to combine your resources with another couple or friends, draw up a contract with the help of an experienced real estate lawyer. At a minimum it should spell out:

☐ Who has use of which parts of the property.
☐ What percentage of the mortgage, maintenance, repair, tax, and utility bills each of you is expected to pay.

- [ ] What percentage of the property each person owns.
- [ ] What happens to a co-owner's share if he or she dies, moves, or cannot meet a share of the payments?
- [ ] How does one co-owner buy out another, and how is the price established?

That's not all, folks

There are a lot more ways to enter the housing market that involve different ways to manipulate your mortgage arrangement. Some of the more successful approaches are discussed in Chapter V.

CHAPTER IV

Finding a house and making a deal

B ack a couple of chapters ago, discussing ways to investigate neighborhoods, we suggested reading newspapers. You're going to be spending a lot of time with the classified real estate sections and most probably a real estate agent. Here's how they both work.

REAL ESTATE ADVERTISING

Both individual home owners and real estate agencies advertise in the local newspapers. Even if you have an agent you love, keep reading the ads. That's the only way you'll see FSBOs (for sale by owner), homes being sold by owners who are saving an agent's commission by selling their houses themselves. If you haven't chosen an agent yet, reading the classifieds will give you a good sense of which ones are most active in the price range and neighborhoods you are looking for.

Over a period of time, the classifieds will also give you a good sense of the market. Are the same houses advertised week after week? Are prices being lowered on any of them? Does it seem that center hall colonials bring a somewhat higher price than split-levels?

Except in areas where there is a law against it, real estate agencies also advertise with "For Sale" signs on the front lawns of houses they are marketing. Usually going up to the house and knocking on the front door will *not* get you inside for a quick tour. Most often, the real estate agency has an agreement with the owner that potential buyers must be accompanied by an agent.

REAL ESTATE AGENTS

Real estate agents are sales people who have taken hours of formal training and passed a written exam given by the state in order to get a license to sell houses. Agents cannot be independent; they must work under the supervision of a licensed real estate broker.

Real estate brokers have survived even more exams. A broker can be an independent business person, hire agents, buy and sell properties, and receive fees and commissions. Many brokers are also Realtors, a registered trademark of the National Association of Realtors (NAR). Brokers who join the association and become Realtors promise to abide by its code of ethics.

Commissions on houses sold by agents are paid to the brokers who employ them, who in turn pay a portion of that commission to the agent. There is a much publicized notion that, because brokers and agents are paid by the seller, they will always favor the seller in any negotiations. But in actual practice, agents tend to be protective of both seller and buyer. After all, if a deal doesn't go through, the agent gets nothing. Furthermore, if you are buying your first house, a good agent will want your business when you decide to sell it and buy your next home.

What real estate agents do for you

Having a good agent on your side is invaluable, especially for a first time-buyer coming into an unfamiliar area. Agents "know the territory." They can save you hours of wasted time by showing you houses in neighborhoods and price ranges that meet your requirements. They can help you negotiate to buy, get a mortgage, find a lawyer, and hire an inspector.

If you aren't comfortable with the first agent assigned to you by the broker you have chosen, ask for another one to be assigned. It is important that you work with an agent you trust and feel is responsive to your needs.

There is no good reason to work with more than one agent in any given area if that area has a Multiple Listing Service (MLS). Wherever MLS is in use, your agent can take you into every house currently for sale in the area. When a house is sold, commissions paid by the seller are divided between the agency marketing the house and the agency working with the buyer.

It is a mistake to think that, because you are dealing with the agency that is marketing the house you want to buy, you may be able to get commissions reduced or make some sort of side deal. It won't happen with a reputable agency.

Some questions to ask

How do you know how competent an agent is? During your first meeting, while he or she is asking you questions about what you are looking for, ask a few questions of your own.

Does your firm belong to a Multiple Listing Service? Most areas, except extremely large cities and remote rural communities, are serviced by an MLS system. The service is supported by dues paid by all of the subscribing agencies in the area it covers. It receives information from all of them each day about every house put up for sale and every house that has been officially sold. It then publishes that information and passes it on to subscribers. Any agency operating in an MLS area that does not subscribe is at a distinct disadvantage.

In New York City and other areas that have no MLS, you may have to consider working with more than one agency. Without MLS, the primary aim of every agent is to find buyers for the houses his or her agency has for sale. In other words, you are at the mercy of what may be a limited inventory.

Do you work full-time? There are exceptions, of course, and you may find a compatible part-time sales person. But it can be annoying to adjust your needs to a part-time schedule, and you know that a full-time sales person depends on the job for his or her livelihood.

Will you negotiate all terms, prices, offers, and counteroffers? If the answer is no, walk away. The emotional aspects of buying a house can be traumatic. You will be able to make much clearer decisions during the buying process if negotiations are conducted through a third party, such as a real estate agent or lawyer. Statistics show that agents across the country consistently negotiate better deals than home buyers can negotiate for themselves.

Can you help find financing, a lawyer, and an inspection firm? The answers will usually be yes. If not, there may be a local law against agents providing some of this assistance. Even so, they can informally recommend lawyers, inspectors, and lenders you can call on.

How to work with an agent

Be open and honest about your needs and wants. Many savvy veteran home buyers recommend that you not tell your agent the absolute maximum amount you are willing to pay. But if you give her or him a range of prices a bit below that maximum, don't play any other games. Most agents will probably show you a variety of house types in different price ranges anyway, to get a sense of what you *really* like and don't like.

A good agent will keep in touch with you regularly and send you information about new houses as soon as they are available. When the agent makes appointments for you to see houses, don't look at more than five or six per trip. Any more than that and everything you see will become one unmemorable blur.

Leave pets and children behind, and let the agent do the

driving. He or she knows the area better than you do, and not driving allows you to observe neighborhoods more closely and ask questions.

Keep giving the agent feedback about what you have seen that you like and dislike. And don't depend on your own memory. After you've seen a number of houses, it's too easy to forget which feature was in which house. Take a camera along (a Polaroid is perfect) and take photos of any house that isn't a complete, absolute impossibility. Take a notepad along, too, and write down your impressions of each house on a single sheet. Do it immediately after you leave. Then attach those notes to the snapshots along with a copy of the agent's listing sheet on the house (this sheet will include information about taxes, utilities, basic features, and asking price). You'll be amazed at how much easier it is to have a rational discussion Sunday night about the dozen houses you've seen over the weekend.

By all means take a knowledgeable friend along, especially if you are visiting a house for the second or third time and want another opinion.

When to look for another agent

Consider switching agents or even agencies if the agent you are working with:

- ☐ Only shows you properties that are listed by his or her agency.
- ☐ Does not regularly send you information about houses in your price range that have come on the market.
- ☐ Keeps showing you houses that are too expensive and rarely shows you one you can afford.
- ☐ Tries to pressure you into making a quick decision.
- ☐ Doesn't level with you about a house or neighborhood. If you find out independently that a neighborhood is on a downward spiral and the agent hasn't told you this, move on to somebody you can trust.

HOW MANY HOUSES SHOULD I LOOK AT?

It isn't really unusual for prospective buyers to fall in love with the first house they see. If that happens to you, make sure you quickly visit at least a dozen comparably priced houses. No one should buy a house without some effort at comparison shopping.

It also isn't unusual for months to go by without seeing anything you like. That's when you begin asking yourselves questions about the priorities you have set and whether they are realistic. There's nothing wrong with changing your mind. Maybe a single-family house with a big yard was your number one priority a few months ago, but the idea of condominium living looks more appealing today. Remember you are buying a *first* house, not necessarily the house you will live in forever.

CHOOSING A LAWYER

It is possible in some parts of the country to purchase a house without the services of a lawyer, but it is seldom a wise decision unless you are an expert on such things as property titles and deed transfers. You are investing many thousands of dollars in this transaction, and the few hundred dollars a knowledgeable attorney will charge will give you the protection you need.

The ideal time to hire a lawyer is just prior to making an offer to buy. Often, the buyer uses the real estate agent to make the offer and, only after agreement on price has been reached, is a lawyer hired. In some states, the lawyer is expected to review the offer before it is presented to the seller. Before you hire a lawyer, ask:

- ☐ What will your fee be?
- ☐ Will your charges be broken down by various tasks performed (helping in the negotiations, writing and reviewing the contract, etc.)? Establish beforehand just what you want your lawyer to do.
- ☐ If the house is bought directly from a seller, without using an agent, will you negotiate terms for us?

- [ ] Will you attend the closing?

Among the services you can expect your attorney to perform:

- [ ] Examine the offer to buy before you sign it.
- [ ] Draft and negotiate the purchase contract.
- [ ] Make certain a proper title search has been conducted and that you receive the property free and clear.
- [ ] Recommend the kind of deed you should have.
- [ ] Recommend how you should take title to the property (joint tenancy, joint tenancy in common, partnership).
- [ ] Review all documents involved in the purchase.
- [ ] Review closing costs and attend the closing.
- [ ] Assist you with any post-purchase problems for an additional fee.

HOW MUCH TO OFFER

When you finally find a house you like, the next step is to make an offer to buy. Your real estate agent can help you determine an opening bid, but the factors that will most influence your first offer to buy include:

How much can you afford to spend? Obvious, but make sure you have also included money for closing costs, moving expenses, and any renovations or repairs you believe are immediately necessary.

How low will the seller be willing to go? The agent will probably know *why* the sellers are moving. If they are simply planning to trade up, they may not be willing to take much less than their asking price. If the main breadwinner has been transferred, they may be in a hurry and willing to negotiate. If they've already purchased another house and time is running out, they may be particularly eager to sell.

How long has the house been on the market? If you are the first bidder on a house that has just been put on the market, the sellers will probably want to wait for someone to come close to their asking price. If the house has been on the market for a long time, they may be more flexible.

When you and your agent have sorted through these questions, you decide on an opening bid. You might pick a number that is in line with, but somewhat below, what similar houses have sold for in the past six months. Your bid figure should in any case be lower than the price you can afford. This will give you some room to negotiate when the seller makes a counteroffer.

THE NEGOTIATIONS

The professionals do it best. They have been in the same situation many times before and are more likely to reach an unemotional agreement that meets everyone's needs. Even with a third party involved, real estate agents describe some negotiations for the purchase of a house as all-out psychological warfare. It helps to have a dispassionate person in the middle.

Once your offer has been tendered, the bargaining begins. If the home owner is willing to negotiate at all, you should quickly receive a counteroffer that is somewhat less than the asking price and more than you have tendered. Of course, you may also be told that the seller believes the house is "priced to sell" and won't consider anything less than a full price offer. Either way, your response will be to either raise your offer or stop negotiating.

How do you know which to do? Unfortunately, just as there is no way to tell if someone is bluffing in a poker game unless you pay to see the cards, there is no way to answer that question. You simply decide how much you want the house and whether you are willing to risk losing it by calling what may be the seller's bluff. Lots of people have waited and saved thousands of dollars because the seller eventually came back. Others have lost a house they wanted and could have had if they had raised their bid by just $1,000.

During the negotiations, keep the seller's priorities as well as your own in mind. Maybe you won't mind paying him more if he'll include some furniture you liked. Maybe she's eager to move quickly and will take a bit less if you can assure her you'll make that possible. Don't bargain for the sake of bargaining.

WORKING WITH AN FSBO (FOR SALE BY OWNER)

If you are buying a house directly from an owner, you won't get any help from a real estate agent. You will have to do your own negotiations, unless you specifically hire a lawyer to handle them. Once you and the owner have come to an agreement, you must hire a lawyer to write the contract. Some things to be aware of when dealing with an FSBO:

- [ ] Be sure of the price range of houses in the area before you make an offer.
- [ ] Verify the property taxes and the annual cost of utilities.
- [ ] Don't go through the house with a real estate agent. You or the seller might become liable, under local law, for a commission on the sale.
- [ ] The owner is saving on real estate commissions by selling direct. At the very least, some of that saving should be reflected in a lower-than-market-value price to you.
- [ ] Get your offer in writing as quickly as possible, so you can be certain that you and the seller are in full agreement.

MAKING AN OFFER TO BUY

In some areas, an offer to buy can be made informally between your agent and the seller's agent with nothing in writing. In most parts of the country, though, the procedure requires either your lawyer or agent to draw up a written offer to purchase or a sales agreement. This becomes a legal and binding document once you and the sellers sign it, but for the moment it is only a formal statement that tells them you wish to purchase their home for a stipulated price, presuming certain conditions are met.

Depending on state laws and local customs, the offer to buy can be quite short or virtually a first draft of the contract, or agreement of sale, that commits both buyer and seller to the deal. Usually, it includes a clause stating that it is invalid unless both parties agree to and sign a mutually acceptable contract within a week or 10 days after the offer is accepted. If this clause is missing, the offer to buy could itself become the contract.

If the offer to buy is written and executed by your real estate agent, the lawyers for you and the seller review it before it becomes binding. In any case, you sign the offer (sometimes called a binder) at the time you tender it (give it to the seller) and give the real estate agent or your lawyer a "good faith" check. The size of the check varies by local laws and customs, but it is typically from $500 to 1 to 2 percent of the amount of the bid you are making. Try to have the check held rather than cashed and deposited. That way there is no delay in having the money returned to you should the deal fall through.

If the offer is accepted, your money is held in an escrow account and becomes part of the cash down payment you give the seller at the time of closing. Try to make sure that the interest on this money accrues to you while it is in escrow.

THE CONTRACT

When a price has finally been agreed upon, often after two or three rounds of offers and counteroffers, the offer is turned into a final contract. Negotiating the details of that contract should be done by your lawyer and the seller's lawyer.

When the lawyers have worked out a sales contract that everyone can agree to, it is signed by you and the seller. You then have a week or so to produce a check for a percentage of the purchase price of the house, minus the "good faith" money put up when you made your offer to buy. This is known as earnest money, and depending on state and local laws, it may be placed in an escrow account that belongs to your lawyer, the seller's lawyer, or one of the real estate agencies involved in the deal. On the day of the closing, it becomes part of what you pay as a down payment.

The contract is legally binding on both you and the seller and commits you to buying the house on certain terms subject to certain contingencies. Typically, it will include:

- [ ] The date the agreement is executed.
- [ ] The full legal names of all buyers and sellers.
- [ ] The address of the property and perhaps a legal description of it.
- [ ] The purchase price of the house and terms of sale, including the closing date.
- [ ] The kind of deed that will be used to convey title of the house to you.
- [ ] A statement about the kind of financing you intend to obtain, including the amount of the mortgage.
- [ ] A statement about how the taxes, insurance, fuel, and other such costs will be prorated between you and the seller.
- [ ] An estimate of the closing costs and a statement of who will pay for what.
- [ ] A list of all furnishings and appliances that aren't attached to the structure of the building but are included in the sale. This could include rugs, chandeliers, and draperies as well as the refrigerator, washer, and dryer. *Be specific.* If the contract calls for a chandelier without stating that it is the antique pewter and crystal heirloom now in the front hall, the seller is free to replace it with a dime store special. One real estate agent still remembers the amazement on the faces of the buyers of one beautifully landscaped house. The seller, an avid gardener, decided that since her favorite flowers and shrubs weren't itemized in the contract, she was free to take them with her.
- [ ] The expiration date of the contract (essentially, how long you have to find your mortgage and have inspections done).
- [ ] An agreement by the seller to keep the property insured until the sale is completed. The amount of the insurance shouldl equal the sales price.
- [ ] In the case of a new house, a statement of all remaining construction work to be done, as well as all other responsibilities of the builder, together with the penalties to be paid if he does not adhere to the agreement.
- [ ] A statement as to who will hold the escrow money and who gets the interest.

☐ A declaration of your right to inspect the property on the day of the closing or immediately before the closing date.

☐ If the sellers are not moving out of the house on or before the day of the closing, a declaration of their moving date along with whatever compensation will be given to the buyer for letting them stay past the closing date. Set as stiff a fee as possible; if you charge a nominal $10 a day, the sellers may be in no hurry to move.

Contingencies

The contract includes a number of contingencies that must be met. Typically, these include such provisions as:

☐ You will be able to get an acceptable mortgage within a specified time period (usually two months), or you have the right to terminate the contract. The seller also has the right to terminate if you don't get your mortgage within the specified period.

☐ The house will be turned over to you in the same condition it was in when the contract was signed.

☐ The property will be conveyed to you free and clear of any liens or encumbrances.

☐ The seller warrants that there are no structural or mechanical defects that you have not been made aware of.

☐ The seller warrants that there are no pending public improvements or assessments you do not know about.

☐ Your right to terminate the contract if a structural inspection conducted by a reputable building engineer discovers more damage than you can accept.

☐ Any termite or radon problems discovered by an inspector will be corrected by the seller at the seller's expense.

☐ The house must be appraised for no less than the purchase price.

Be certain that all contingencies are clearly stated in the contract and that each will be satisfied within a specified period of time. Also, be sure there is a clear statement to the effect that if any contingency is not met, the contract is null and void, and you get your deposit money back.

Real life, real answers.

For three days after they made their first bid on the four-bedroom colonial house in a Cleveland suburb, David and Noreen Fairchild waited anxiously for some kind of response from the sellers. Their real estate agent thought that the sellers, who were retiring and had already bought a condominium in New Mexico, were anxious to make a deal.

The asking price was $160,000. The agent recommended that the Fairchilds start at $148,000, which was well below the $155,000 she thought the house was worth.

When the counteroffer came back, reducing the asking price by $5,000, the agent's advice was to take it. But David wasn't sure. He asked her to bid $150,000. This time, the response came back quickly; the sellers didn't feel they could go below $155,000.

The house contained some handsome dining room furniture that both David and Noreen had admired. Guessing that the furniture wouldn't fit in the New Mexico condo, the Fairchilds asked that it be included in the sale, and they bid $152,000

When a final price of $154,000 was agreed upon, the furniture was part of the deal.

In some cases you may have to do some more negotiating with the seller. Suppose the engineering report states that the roof must be replaced. Who pays for this? It can be argued either way. Often the result is that the seller reduces the price by half the estimated cost of the repair, and you pay the other half out of pocket.

HOUSE INSPECTIONS

Many communities require that every house that changes owners must have a Certificate of Occupancy. When the house is sold, the seller must notify the proper authorities and make an appointment for an inspection. A Certificate of Occupancy inspection is typically concerned with the safety of the building's occupants; it is rarely a rigorous inspection of the structure. The housing inspector either issues a Certificate of Occupancy or requires the seller to make certain changes. For example, local laws may require smoke detectors, and a Certificate of Occupancy would be withheld until detectors were installed.

Engineering inspections

There are plenty of other ways to save money when you are purchasing your first home. *Don't* scrimp when it comes to getting a structural evaluation of the building. An engineering inspection of an average house will cost between $200 and $500 and it is worth every penny. Houses have not gone to closing because the engineering inspection turned up severe structural flaws that the owners were unaware of.

Termite inspections

If the house is in an area where termites or carpenter ants are even a remote possibility, make sure that one of the contingencies in the contract is that the house pass a termite inspection. Spotting damage from termites isn't always easy, because they do their damage by eating the wood inside the walls. Some engineering inspections include a termite inspection, but make sure you get one.

Radon

These days it seems there's always something new to worry about. But in many parts of the country, radon, a radioactive gas that occurs naturally and emanates from the earth, has become a real concern. In high concentrations and with long exposure, it can increase the risks of developing lung cancer. Fortunately, most houses have a very low radon concentration, and a high concentration can usually be remedied. In areas where high concentrations of radon are prevalent, many sellers have had inspections done; in that case, the owner can document the house's radon level. Otherwise, have an inspection done yourself. If the concentration is high, remedial steps such as ventilating the basement can be expensive.

APPRAISALS

House and termite inspections are not mandatory in most parts of the country, although lending institutions require them in some areas. But lenders often send their own appraisers to investigate a house they are considering financing.

Appraisers look at a house in terms of its overall worth, not at details such as whether the plumbing is in peak working order. They also evaluate the neighborhood (location, location, and location) and send a report back to the lender explaining their opinion of the property's worth on the open market.

On rare occasions, the appraised value of a house will be lower than the amount of the mortgage loan you have applied for. If this happens, you have four choices:

☐ Have your lawyer or real estate agent ask for a second appraisal.

☐ Ask your lawyer or agent to negotiate a lower sales price in line with the appraisal.

☐ Increase the size of your down payment by enough to make up the difference between the sales price and the mortgage.

☐ Cancel the contract to buy the house.

AFTER THE INSPECTIONS

With the exception of the lender's appraisal, inspections usually take place within a week or two after the contract has been signed. But even before the inspections are completed, you should begin shopping for a mortgage loan.

CHAPTER V

Finding the right mortgage

W hen you borrow money from a lender to purchase your house, that house is pledged by you as security for the repayment of the loan. Until the loan plus the interest that has accrued on it is repaid in full, the lender will have a lien on your property. That means that the lender has the right to take possession of the property (foreclose on it) if you don't repay on schedule.

Considering that a mortgage loan can last as long as 30 years and cost hundreds of thousands of dollars, it's no wonder that many first-time home buyers lose sleep even thinking about making such a commitment. But millions of people have survived the process, and you will, too.

Your goal is to find the mortgage loan at the lowest possible interest rate with the terms most advantageous to you. The way to find it is to *shop* for it, as you would for any other product, comparing what is available from many different lenders.

There are several types of mortgage loans to choose from, and the more popular ones are discussed later in this chapter. But first it is useful to know the different lenders you can approach for a mortgage.

WHERE THE MONEY IS

Your real estate agent and perhaps your lawyer can suggest local lenders who are currently active in your area. Certainly don't disregard your own bank if you have maintained an account there for any length of time. Lenders are most comfortable with people they know.

Keep in mind that in a normal real estate market, mortgage lenders are in competition with each other. As difficult as it may be to believe during your talks with some lenders, they actually do want to make mortgage loans. If you qualify for the mortgage you are looking for, you are a valued potential customer. That's true no matter which of these different kinds of lenders is involved.

Savings and loan associations

The primary purpose of S&Ls, or thrifts as they are sometimes known, has traditionally been to provide residential mortgages. That makes them a logical place to start when you look for a loan. In the East, mutual savings banks are near clones of S&Ls. In either case, it may help if you have a savings account in the institution you intend to approach, although this is certainly not mandatory.

Commercial banks

The days are long gone when banks loaned money only to businesses. Most commercial banks, including the largest ones, such as Citibank and the Bank of America, now compete with other lenders for residential mortgages.

Credit unions

Credit unions are owned by their depositors, each of whom holds a number of shares in the union that is in direct proportion to the amount of money in his or her savings account. You can't approach a credit union for a mortgage loan unless you belong to one, but if you do, you have an excellent chance of finding a loan at very competitive rates.

Other financial institutions

More and more nonbanking companies are getting into the

home mortgage business. General Motors, for example, offers mortgages through its General Motors Acceptance Corporation, and the Sears Mortgage Company will sometimes approve a housing loan even before you find a house. On occasion, some of these new financing corporations have applied less stringent criteria to borrowers than their competitors, so if you are having trouble finding a lender among the older financial institutions, try the newer ones.

Loan correspondents

Even the largest lending institutions don't have the facilities to make mortgage loans in every area of the country. In many cases they work with a local agent, or loan correspondent, who provides them with a knowledge of the local real estate market and economic conditions. Loan correspondents are either mortgage brokers or mortgage bankers, and you may encounter them through a referral by your real estate agent. They are often able to find mortgage money during times of tight money.

Sellers

When money is scarce and mortgages are hard to get from financial institutions, home owners will sometimes take back a mortgage in order to sell. Or you may be able to buy from an owner who is retiring and looking for a consistent source of income. In effect, such sellers continue to control their houses: if there is a default on mortgage payments, the house reverts to them.

Builders

If you are buying a newly constructed house from a builder, he will probably have made arrangements with a lender to finance mortgages for qualified buyers.

TYPES OF MORTGAGES

There are a variety of traditional as well as new types of

mortgage loans available to borrowers today, with more appearing every day. In fact, keeping track of all of your options can be extremely difficult. But most good real estate agents are aware of what types are available in their areas and they can be invaluable in steering you to lenders who can best meet your needs. The different types of mortgages described on the next few pages are currently the most popular options in most parts of the country.

Fixed-rate mortgages (FRMs)

Until fairly recently, the only type of mortgage generally available was fixed rate, usually with a 30-year term. With a fixed-rate mortgage you make regular monthly payments based on a guaranteed interest rate that doesn't change during the duration of the loan. The payment in the first year is the same as the payment in the last year. The normal term of an FRM is still 30 years, but you can get them written for 10, 15, 20, 25, or even 40 years. Generally, lenders require a 20 percent down payment with an FRM. If you get an FHA (Federal Housing Administration) insured loan or buy PMI (private mortgage insurance), you may be able to reduce your down payment to as little as 5 percent. (More on mortgage insurance later in this chapter.)

Adjustable-rate mortgages (ARMs)

This type of mortgage loan adjusts the interest rate at regular intervals either up or down, depending on the movement of whatever index (such as the current interest rate on U.S. Treasury bills) the lender has specified in your agreement. The term of an ARM can be anywhere up to 30 years; currently, interest rates are adjusted at six-month, one-year, or three-year intervals.

ARMs have a cap—a ceiling—on how high the interest rate and/or the monthly payment can go during the term of a loan. They usually specify how great a change upward can be made in any single adjustment period. One common cap is a "two-six,"

Real life, real answers.

F rank Boyle was a high school social studies teacher in San Francisco when he met Betty Lange, a registered nurse from Kentucky. Within a year, he surprised his Bay Area friends by trading a $25,000-a-year salary for a $17,500 one in a Louisville school. Frank, 27, and Betty, 29, got married a week before Frank's first school year began.

Together, the Boyles make $33,000 a year; neither had saved any money before their marriage, and they now have just $3,000 in savings. Can that be enough for a down payment on a house?

They've looked at some houses, and to Frank's astonishment, about $50,000 will buy a pleasant three-bedroom house within walking distance of his school and just five miles from the hospital where Betty works. A real estate broker tells them they can get an FHA mortgage and works the numbers out with them:

FHA-appraised value of house (also market price)	$48,000
3% down payment; therefore loan amount (97% of $48,000)	46,560
Down payment required	$1,440
FHA closing costs (schedule subject to change)	1,200
Estimated legal fees and other miscellaneous costs	500
Cash needed	$3,140

Monthly charges:	
30-year, fixed-rate mortgage @ 10.5%	$426
Taxes @ $1,200 a year	100
Insurance @ $180 a year	15
Monthly PITI	$541

With a combined salary of $33,000 a year, the Boyles can afford a monthly PITI of $770. So the house is well within their budget.

meaning that the rate can't go higher than 2 percent in one year or 6 percent over the life of the mortgage.

Typically, ARM lenders offer a beginning rate from one to three percentage points below the going rate for an FRM and set a cap that is a few points above that going rate.

Obviously, ARMs are inherently riskier than FRMs. It is impossible for anyone to predict where interest rates will be in a year, much less in 20 years. Remember that ARMs came into being because *lenders* wanted protection from being locked into a low fixed rate during periods of high inflation and high interest rates.

During a period when interest rates are extremely high by historical standards, ARMs can be a good bet. But an FRM is usually the most conservative choice. If you do decide on an ARM, make sure you have figured out what your maximum payment will be in a worst-case scenario.

One worst-case scenario, if you get an ARM with a cap on the monthly payment but not on the interest rate, is the possibility that the monthly payment may not cover the revised interest charges. In other words, the interest rate could rise to the point where interest payments alone exceed the monthly payment you are required to make. In such a case, you could actually find yourself making maximum monthly payments while the total amount of your debt increased!

A cap on the interest rate rather than a cap on the monthly payment will avoid this potential problem, but, again, figure out how much your maximum payment could be before taking out the loan.

Generally, it is better for you if an ARM is adjusted every three years instead of more frequently. And, obviously, you want the lowest maximum cap possible.

Convertible mortgages

These are ARMs with a significant difference. They allow you to convert the ARM to an FRM at a specified time in the duration of the mortgage, sometimes at the time of the first adjustment, sometimes later. You would convert, of course, if interest rates were escalating, and you wanted to lock in a fixed rate for the remainder of the term of the loan. There is always a conversion fee involved, but it is invariably less than the cost of refinancing.

Not all lenders offer this convertible option, and those that do, peg their rates to different indices. Ask which index your lender will use.

Graduated payment mortgages (GPMs)

GPMs are a gamble on future increases in your income. They were designed for young people who can reasonably expect their incomes to rise over the first few years of the loan. A GPM can be either an FRM or an ARM, but it always calls for lower monthly payments at the beginning of the loan that gradually increase during the first five or ten years. At that point, payments level off for the remaining term of the loan.

Ultimately, a GPM can cost more than standard FRMs or ARMs because there is more chance for "negative amortization," the worst-case scenario described above. Some fixed-rate GPMs, in fact, call for negative amortization in the first years; this means you would actually continue to add to the principal amount owed on the mortgage until your monthly payment is increased. In such a case, the lender might require a down payment higher than 20 percent.

Growing equity mortgages (GEMs)

Monthly payments are fixed with a GEM, but each year they are increased by a specified percentage, such as 4 percent. This annual "overpayment" is applied to the principal you owe, so that a 30-year, fixed-rate mortgage could be paid off in 15 or 20 years.

Balloon mortgages

Fixed monthly payments are calculated as if the loan were to be paid off in 20 or 30 years, but those payments are made only for three, five, or 10 years. At that point, the mortgage "balloons"— the principal remaining on the loan comes due. You have to refinance—find another mortgage loan—elsewhere.

Why would anyone choose such a loan? If you are certain you will be transferred out of the area in seven or eight years, or if you know your children will be gone and you'll want a smaller house, a 10-year balloon on a 40-year mortgage can help you hold monthly payments down.

Shared-equity mortgages

Lenders provide this type of loan when you have an investor, such as a parent, who will not live in the house but will put up all or part of the down payment and/or pay part of the monthly payments. You enter a partnership with this outside investor, and you are each allowed tax deductions proportional to your share of monthly payments.

Suppose you buy in an area where housing is appreciating, and you have a well-to-do uncle looking for a long-term investment. In return for half of the down payment from him, you might agree that some percentage of your gain on the house will go to him when it is sold.

A shared-equity mortgage is a potential source of emotional strife, especially if the outside investor is a family member. Make certain that you have a comprehensive legal agreement that covers all the possibilities, including death, divorce, and bankruptcy.

SELLER FINANCING

Sellers can often help a buyer purchase a home, even when lending institutions consider the buyer too high a risk. In such cases, the seller becomes the lender and determines the amount of the down payment and the interest rate to be paid on the money borrowed. That rate is likely to be higher than current levels from other lenders, but the buyer will save on points (see next chapter), and closing costs may be greatly reduced.

Because the seller can treat the monthly payments as an installment sale, he is taxed only on the money he receives each year. And in all cases, the seller has the same lien against the property as any other lender would have; he gets it back if you default on the loan.

There are several ways that finding the right seller might help you.

Assumptions

If the seller has an assumable mortgage (a loan in which the agreement states that the borrower is allowed to let a third party assume his or her contractual obligations), you can take over the seller's monthly payments, often at an interest rate below the current going rate. The problem usually is that the difference between the remaining principal owed on the assumable mortgage and the price of the house is far too large to be covered in a down payment. In such a case, the seller might be willing to become a second mortgage lender.

Most fixed-rate mortgages are not assumable. Most ARMs and FHA- and VA-approved mortgages are.

Second mortgages

Suppose the seller lets you assume his mortgage, you give him the largest down payment possible, and you are still $30,000 short of the purchase price. You can make up the difference with a second mortgage.

There's no difference between first and second mortgages except that, in case of default, the holder of the second mortgage doesn't get his money until after the holder of the first mortgage gets his. Because of this, lending institutions are reluctant to write second mortgages; when they do, the loans will have a higher interest rate and a shorter term than a first mortgage. You might be able to get the seller to give you a second mortgage. Just be sure you can afford the combined total of monthly payments.

Wraparounds

Wraparounds are a variation on second mortgages. They tie the seller's old financing into the buyer's new financing. Even after the house is sold, the seller continues to make his monthly mortgage payments. At the same time he lends you the difference between your down payment and the purchase price of the house.

Suppose he had a $50,000 balance left on his mortgage at an 8 percent rate. He gives you a wraparound loan for $75,000 at 11 percent. You make payments to him, he makes payments to his original lender, and he pockets the difference. Wraparounds can be advantageous to both buyer and seller, but you have to be extra careful about getting good legal advice before you agree to one.

Buy-downs

The buy-down is essentially an interest rate subsidy made by the seller, usually, but not always, the builder of a new house. The seller pays the lender up-front cash to lower the borrower's interest rates. A buy-down can be either permanent or temporary. In a permanent buy-down, the interest rate might be reduced by as much as 1 percent throughout the term of the loan. More common are temporary buy-downs, in which the interest rate is reduced by 3 percent the first year, 2 percent the second year, and 1 percent the third year.

MORTGAGE INSURANCE

If you can't afford to put up a substantial (usually 20 percent) down payment on your house, you will be required by the lender to purchase mortgage insurance. There are two kinds: government-backed and private.

Private (PMI)

The majority of conventional loans are insured by a private mortgage insurance (PMI) company. These companies guarantee the lenders that, if you default, they will be paid the full amount then owed on the loan. Note that this has nothing at all to do with the personal term life insurance some people buy to pay the lender the remainder of the loan in case of their death. That insurance protects their family, making the house theirs, free and clear; PMI protects the lender.

How much you'll pay for PMI depends on how large a down payment you are able to make, the type of mortgage being insured, and both general and local economic conditions. Generally, it will equal about .40 percent of the mortgage for the first year, with an annual renewal rate of approximately .34 percent of the amount of the loan each year thereafter. Some policies are written so that premiums are sharply reduced or eliminated when your equity in the property becomes high enough.

Federal Housing Administration (FHA)

The Federal Housing Administration (FHA) is an agency of the Department of Housing and Urban Development (HUD). Contrary to some popular misconceptions, it does not lend money to buy homes, but it does insure loans made by lenders. FHA-insured loans are made by approved FHA lenders (most lenders qualify), and anyone can apply for one. Since FHA loans are meant to help buyers with low or moderate incomes, there are limits on the amount of the loan. Currently, and subject to periodic change, depending on what area of the country you live in, the maximum loan amount ranges from $67,500 to $101,250.

To qualify for an FHA loan, you must meet strict requirements about monthly payments as a percentage of your income and have a good credit history. The property you want to buy will also have to meet FHA requirements. But if all the requirements are met, you can get an FHA-insured loan with a minimal down payment, sometimes as low as 3 percent of the purchase price. Just as with PMI, you'll be charged a fee for the insurance, which will be included in your monthly payment.

Interest rates and other terms of the loan are set by the lender, not by the FHA as they once were. If you think you may qualify for an FHA loan, discuss it with potential lenders.

Veterans Administration(VA)

The Veterans Administration (VA) guarantees low or no down payment loans for the purchase of a home if you are a veteran, or the surviving spouse of a veteran, who served at least 181 days on active duty. You can check your eligibility at any regional VA office or by writing to the Veterans Benefits Office (2033 M Street N.W., Washington, DC 20421).

You must meet VA credit requirements, but the formula used is easier to satisfy than those used in conventional loans. There is a one-time 1 percent loan origination fee plus other closing costs that are VA approved. The longest loan period offered by the VA is 30 years. Like FHA loans, VA loans are assumable.

Currently, and subject to change, the VA guarantees veterans a maximum of $37,500 of loan insurance. Because lenders will usually grant up to four times the amount of VA entitlement, you may be able to take out a mortgage for as much as $144,000 if you meet the lender's standards. And if both you and your spouse are veterans, you can combine VA entitlements to increase the mortgage limit.

POINTS AND OTHER LENDER FEES

Unfortunately, no discussion of mortgages of any kind is complete without mentioning points. A point is equal to 1 percent of the principal amount of your loan. If you are borrowing $75,000, a point is $750. Lenders in most parts of the country charge up-front points—actually a kind of prepaid interest—when they make the loan; it is payable by you at the closing. In addition, all lenders charge an up-front loan origination fee, typically 1 to 1.5 percent of the principal amount, to cover all of the paperwork and administrative costs that go into processing a loan.

Make sure you know what points and up-front costs are involved when you talk to lenders. It is not uncommon to find a loan with a slightly higher interest rate that is a better deal than a loan with high up-front costs and heavy point charges.

BUILDING EQUITY FASTER

In Chapter I, there was a brief demonstration of how interest rates and the term of your loan impact on your monthly payment and total interest charges. The obvious advantage of any short-term loan is that your equity in the house builds up more quickly; the faster you pay off the loan, the less interest you will pay. If you anticipate a major expense in less than 30 years, such as a college education for your child, you have a particularly good reason to complete mortgage payments before then. And if you intend to trade up to another house in a few years, the more equity you have, the easier trading up will be.

There are drawbacks to a short-term mortgage. Not only are the monthly payments for short loans higher; down payment requirements may be higher as well. The table on page 75 shows the large differences in the total amounts you will repay a lender during three different loan terms for a fixed-rate mortgage of $80,000 at 11 percent.

If you want to build equity quickly and reduce total interest payments, there are three typical ways to do it.

Fifteen-year mortgages

Usually you can get a slightly lower interest rate on a 15-year mortgage than you would if the term were 30 years. Note that the monthly payments are not as drastically different as you might think. The difference in the $80,000 fixed-rate mortgage at 11 percent illustrated on page 75 is just $147.42 a month.

Biweekly fixed-rate mortgages

You can build equity rapidly by paying your lender half the standard monthly payments every two weeks. This will work out to 13 payments a year instead of 12, and you will pay off the loan years earlier, depending on the interest rate.

You can usually get a lender to go along with a biweekly payment schedule no matter what kind of mortgage you have, including a 15-year loan. However, there is a lot of extra paperwork involved, so don't be surprised if your lender insists that payment be automatically deducted from your bank account every other week.

Extra payments

The simplest and maybe the best way to pay off a loan more quickly is to make added payments on the principal every month you can afford to. If you do this regularly, equity builds up rapidly. Just make clear to the lender that you want the extra money applied to the *principal* on your loan. The best part about paying this way is that you are not locked into paying additional money every month; you can skip an additional payment anytime you like.

SHOPPING FOR A MORTGAGE

Your grandfather may have walked into a savings and loan association, told the loan officer he had had a savings account with them for 15 years, and walked out with a 4 percent fixed-rate mortgage. *Every* S&L in the area back then offered the same terms and the same interest rate. But those halcyon days are over. Today, anyone who doesn't shop for a mortgage is missing a chance to save many thousands of dollars.

You'll recall that an earlier chapter recommended that you have a preliminary meeting, before you look for a house, with at least one lender to discuss local conditions and your own needs

SHORT-TERM VERSUS LONG-TERM LOANS

Fixed-rate mortgage of $80,000 at 11%

	15-year loan	25-year loan	30-year loan
Monthly payments:	$909.28	$784.09	$761.86
Amount owed after:			
5 years	$66,009	$75,964	$77,732
10 years	41,820	68,986	73,819
15 years	Paid	56,921	67,029
20 years		36,063	55,306
25 years		Paid	35,038
30 years			Paid
Total Amount Paid	$163,670	$235,227	$274,269
Total Interest Paid	$83,670	$152,227	$194,269

and qualifications. But when it comes time to seriously compare what's available, you can do most of your early shopping by telephone. When you call a lender, ask to speak to someone about a new mortgage. Tell that person you are buying a home and need information about financing. Remember you are the customer and the lender wants to sell you his product—the loan. Be courteous and pleasant, but make sure you get understandable answers to your questions.

Shopping for a mortgage can be bewildering unless you go about it in an organized manner. Make photocopies of the worksheet on pages 76 and 77 and insert the pertinent data you get from each lender. Talk to at least four or five lenders. Call back and clarify any confusing points. When you are through, you should have narrowed your search to two or three lenders whom you will want to visit and perhaps make applications with.

None of this makes sense unless you have been realistic about how much you can afford and what a lender can reasonably be expected to offer you. By this point you should also have a good idea of whether you want a fixed- or adjustable-rate mortgage. There is no "best mortgage" for everyone, and you—along with your advisers—are ultimately going to have to decide what's best for you.

LENDER INFORMATION WORKSHEET

Name of lending institution _____

Address _____

Phone # _____ Contact/title _____

Types of financing offered (ARMs, FRMs, FHA, VA, PMI)

_____

Fixed-rate mortgage: Interest rate _____

Term _____

ARM _____ Interest rate _____

ARM caps 1st year _____ 2nd year _____

Maximum interest _____

Term _____

Other _____

Features _____ Interest rate _____

Caps _____ Maximum amount of interest _____

Term _____

Other _____

Features _____ Interest rate _____

Caps _____ Maximum amount of interest _____

Term _____

Does the required down payment vary for different types? _____

If I make a larger down payment, can I get a lower interest rate? _____

Minimum down payment _____

Maximum amount of loan _____

Prepayment penalty _____

Late payment penalty _____

Points _____ Who pays? (buyer/seller) _____

Qualifications for loan _____

_____

When will I qualify? _____

Can I include a home improvement loan as part of this mortgage? _____

Can I add to the mortgage to cover closing costs? _____

Can the mortgage be assumed? _____

Length of loan commitment (days) _____

Is this renewable? _____

Is the rate guaranteed? _____

Fees:

Loan origination fee _____

Application fee _____

Appraisal fee _____

Credit check fee _____

Other fees _____

When are fees payable? Application _____ Approval _____ Closing _____

What are the closing costs? _____

Any preferred customer benefits? _____

Additional comments _____

_____

PAYING OFF A MORTGAGE

It takes a long time before your payments on the principal equal or exceed your payments on the interest. Here is how the first year of payments looks on a $75,000 30-year, fixed-rate mortgage at 11%:

Payment	Principal	Interest	Balance Due
0			$75,000.00
1	$26.74	$687.50	$74,973.26
2	$26.99	$687.25	$74,946.27
3	$27.24	$687.01	$74,919.03
4	$27.48	$686.76	$74,891.55
5	$27.74	$686.51	$74,863.81
6	$27.99	$686.25	$74,835.82
7	$28.25	$686.00	$74,807.57
8	$28.51	$685.74	$74,779.07
9	$28.77	$685.47	$74,750.30
10	$29.03	$685.21	$74,721.27
11	$29.30	$684.94	$74,691.97
12	$29.57	$684.68	$74,662.41

After 15 years—half the term of the loan—you are still paying far more interest each month than principal.

180	$136.95	$577.29	$62,840.44
181	$138.21	$576.04	$62,702.24
182	$139.47	$574.77	$62,562.77
183	$140.75	$573.49	$62,422.02
184	$142.04	$572.20	$62,279.97
185	$143.34	$570.90	$62,136.63
186	$144.66	$569.59	$61,991.97
187	$145.98	$568.26	$61,845.99
188	$147.32	$566.92	$61,698.67
189	$148.67	$565.57	$61,550.00
190	$150.03	$564.21	$61,399.97
191	$151.41	$562.83	$61,248.56
192	$152.80	$561.45	$61,095.76

Finally, in the twenty-third year of the loan, interest and principal payments are equal.

277	$331.87	$382.38	$41,381.97
278	$334.91	$379.33	$41,047.06
279	$337.98	$376.26	$40,709.09
280	$341.08	$373.17	$40,368.01
281	$344.20	$370.04	$40,023.81
282	$347.36	$366.88	$39,676.45
283	$350.54	$363.70	$39,325.91
284	$353.76	$360.49	$38,972.15
285	$357.00	$357.24	$38,615.16
286	$360.27	$353.97	$38,254.89
287	$363.57	$350.67	$37,891.31
288	$366.91	$347.34	$37,524.41

From here on, principal payments escalate rapidly.

APPROVAL AND COSTS

When you apply for a mortgage, the lender is required by a federal law (RESPA, the Real Estate Settlement Procedures Act) to give you an estimate of what your closing or settlement costs are likely to be. After the lender notifies you that your loan has been approved (within two weeks of application for a conventional mortgage; up to three months for a VA or FHA loan), he is required to disclose the annual percentage rate (APR) of your loan. Because of the fees and points charged, this APR will always be higher than the interest rate in your mortgage loan contract.

Before you get to the closing, make sure you, your lawyer, and your agent have all checked the lender's documents to be sure the final terms are the same ones you successfully negotiated in the first place.

CHAPTER VI

The closing

T he closing, or settlement as it is called in some areas, occurs four to six weeks after you have a commitment for a mortgage. The date of closing is set by the lender and agreed to by you and the seller, but this can be changed by either party if necessary.

Should you want to move into the house before the closing, you may be able to reach an agreement to pay the seller rent for that period. By the same token, if the seller has not vacated the house by the time of the closing, he must pay you a daily or weekly rental fee until he moves. Make this fee higher than the price of a motel to encourage the seller to vacate the house. You should not move any of your furniture or boxes into the house before the closing unless you have the seller's permission and the assurance that your possessions will be covered under the seller's homeowners insurance.

Closings were once infamous for the shock of unexpected costs, but the government took much of the surprise out of the ordeal with the Real Estate Settlement Procedures Act (RESPA). In addition to the estimate lenders must give you when you apply for a loan, you are also entitled to an itemized breakdown of costs no later than 24 hours before you close. Knowing in advance exactly what you will pay may soften the shock, but, for most people, the closing is still an emotional and rather nerve-wracking event.

The setting of the closing varies depending on the part of the country. On the West Coast it will probably take place in a small office with a single escrow agent. In other places it might be at a law office or in a bank conference room crowded with you, the seller, the two lawyers, the real estate agent, a representative from the title company, and your mortgage lender. Whatever the scene, by the end of the closing, ownership of the home will formally be transferred from the seller to you.

Between the time you have gone to contract on the house and the closing day, there are things you must do to ensure that the transfer will go smoothly.

THE "WALK THROUGH" INSPECTION

The contract you sign should include a clause that allows an inspection of the house a few days before the closing. Even if you won't have a chance to do it in person, include this clause. Perhaps a friend or your lawyer can make the inspection. This "walk through" is necessary to make sure that there have been no major changes in the house: no limbs have fallen through the roof, the lawn has been cut, and everything inside is as you expected it to be. It also ensures that all the personal property included in the sale and specified in the contract is in fact there. Even if the seller is your best, most trusted friend, a moving company might inadvertently have taken something that was supposed to be yours.

Most contracts also include a clause stating that the house will be left "broom clean." This does not mean you will be able to eat off the floors, or even that those floors won't have a bit of dust on them. What it does mean is that all the trash and debris of the previous owner, along with all the things you *didn't* want left in the house, will in fact be removed. If there is still agreed-upon cleaning work to be done, this can be discussed at the closing.

THE TITLE SEARCH

Between the time of the contract and the closing, your lawyer

Real life, real answers.

Jack and Betty Hoban had been looking for a three-bedroom house priced at $100,000 for months when they finally found what they were looking for—a Cape Cod in decent shape for sale by a Mrs. Leech, a widow who was moving to a condominium unit in the same town. Mrs. Leech would not lower her price below $105,000—a stretch for the Hobans even with a gift of money from Betty's parents—but she agreed to include a number of items from the house as part of the purchase price. These were two beds, a sofa, a washer and dryer, a lawn mower, a garden cart, and various tools that had belonged to Mr. Leech. She also agreed to clean the cellar and remove all the boxes, magazines, and discarded household goods that had been accumulating there.

When the Hobans inspected the house three days before the closing, they were dismayed to find that the items included in the house sale were not there, and the basement was untouched. Mrs. Leech's son, unaware of the details of the sale, had taken everything in the house. The specific items included were returned and the son agreed to clean the basement. It wasn't done before the closing, though, so the Hobans ended up doing a lot of it themselves just so they could move in their own belongings.

will order a title search. A title search, conducted by a title insurance company, is an examination of all the public records about who has owned the property you are buying. Especially if you are buying a home in an area that has been settled since colonial days, the search can produce a fascinating historical document. But its purpose is to note any and all encumbrances, liens, mortgages, easements, restrictions, etc., that affect your property and, most importantly, to establish that title to the property—actual ownership—can indeed be legally passed by the sellers to you.

Who pays for the title search depends on local custom, but this should be specified in the contract. If it's your responsibility, and you can find out which firm did the title search for the seller, you may save some money, since there are already records showing the history of the property up to the time the current owners bought it.

TITLE INSURANCE

Even after the title has been searched and verified, the lender will require you to carry title insurance. Title insurance protects the *lender's* interest in your property in case some unfound or missing claim to the property shows up before you finish paying off the loan. If you want to protect yourself as well, you should consider taking out additional insurance.

Sometimes it is possible to save money on the policy by renewing the seller's title insurance at what is known as a reissue rate, as opposed to taking out a totally new policy.

Many states allow title insurance companies, rather than lawyers, to close the sale of a house. If you are buying in such an area, your lawyer will eventually turn over the task of completing the closing to the title insurance company. At that point there will be no more need for the lawyer's services.

MORTGAGE SURVEY

In addition to the title search, the mortgage lender might also order a mortgage survey. This certifies that the house you are buying is located within the boundaries designated on an official survey map of the area. It also defines the boundary lines of the property and states whether or not any part of that property encroaches on, or is encroached upon, by any lot adjoining it. If there is an encroachment or easement that has not been noted, your lawyer can negotiate some sort of settlement with the seller.

HOMEOWNERS INSURANCE

At the closing, you will be required to show that you have taken out homeowners insurance. If you do not take out your own, the lender will automatically add a policy to your loan, and you will be charged accordingly.

There are several types of homeowners insurance with several levels of protection, but basically you want a policy that covers at least 80 percent of the replacement cost of the house. Furnishings, clothes, etc. are additional. If you are buying a condominium, you will need to pay for two policies; one for your own unit and a prorated share of one for the entire condominium complex. The latter is included in your monthly maintenance fee payment. Read it, compare it with your own policy, and make sure there isn't a gap in coverage—something not covered by either policy.

When you take out homeowners insurance, you may elect to take a number of options with the basic policy, but an option you definitely want states that the company will periodically give you the right to increase your coverage. Exercising this right will not increase your premiums by very much, and it could mean a big difference should anything happen to your house.

UTILITIES

You don't want to move into a house without heat or light. Call a couple of weeks beforehand and ask to have electric, gas, and water meters read on the day of the closing. At the same time, have accounts in your name start on the same day.

If the house has oil heat, have the oil company measure what's in the tank or come to some other agreement with the seller.

CLOSING DAY

Closings can be sedate affairs that take less than an hour or they can become long, drawn-out hassles. If all goes as expected, you are there basically to sign checks. Everybody else is there to receive your checks. The lawyers are there to settle

Real life, real answers.

Ray and Celia Cartwright bought their first home in 1978 in a quiet suburb 20 miles west of Milwaukee. They made some handsome renovations to their home over the years, redoing the kitchen and putting in a second bath. During the energy crunch, Ray bought a wood-burning stove and installed it in the family room. Without question, the stove added charm to the room. Better still, it was so efficient it cut their annual heating bill nearly in half.

The Cartwrights used the stove steadily for five years. Ray forgot that he was supposed to clean the chimney every two years to keep the buildup of creosote from becoming a hazard. One cold night, two hours after he banked the fire in the stove when they went to bed, the creosote in the chimney erupted. By the time the smoke alarms woke Ray and Celia and they called the fire department, the house was beyond saving.

The Cartwrights were fully insured; their policy stated that they would be paid 80 percent of the cost of rebuilding their home. But the rate schedule was based on 1978 prices because Celia had always thought the insurance company was just trying to make more money every time it gave them the option to increase their coverage. By 1990, the worth of the house had tripled and the cost of its reconstruction was easily twice what it had been 10 years before. The amount of money the Cartwrights received from their insurance policy barely paid for cleaning up the debris and framing a new house.

any last-minute disputes that may arise, to be sure that all the documents are fully and accurately completed, and to make certain that all the people who have money coming to them are paid.

CLOSING DOCUMENTS

A number of documents will be processed at the closing.

Though not all of these will be applicable in all areas, the main documents usually are:

- ☐ Settlement statements. One for the buyer and one for the seller, these show the monies due.
- ☐ A copy of the loan commitment letter. This will specify the details of the loan, and can be referred to in case there is a discrepancy.
- ☐ The contract to purchase.
- ☐ The deed. This transfers title.
- ☐ Proof of homeowners insurance and other insurance policies that might be required. Bring the policies and photocopies showing the first month or first quarter payment to the insurance company. You might not be able to close without these documents.
- ☐ Mortgage and/or deed of trust. Both of these documents include a description of the property, the monies to be paid, and the amount and schedule of regular payments.
- ☐ Assumption statement. This gives the details in cases where the existing mortgage is taken over by the buyer. Even when the buyer is assuming the seller's mortgage, a title search will be required.
- ☐ Releases. These documents show that any liens or judgments against the property have been paid.
- ☐ Lien waiver. This protects the lender against any judgments against the property.
- ☐ Inspection contingencies. These documents affirm that the various inspections of the house have been completed and that no problems regarding termites, structural problems, or radon are present.

CLOSING FEES

Make sure you have brought enough checks, and make sure there is adequate money in your checking account for contingencies. Most of the fees listed below will be your responsibility. You might be required to bring a certified check for some of them; your lawyer will tell you if this is necessary.

These are the main fees to be paid:

- ☐ Loan origination fee. This covers the lender's expenses incurred in processing the loan.
- ☐ Points. A point is 1 percent of the mortgage, so on a $50,000 mortgage, a point is $500. Depending on the lender and the type of mortgage you get, you will usually be required to pay one to three points at the closing unless you have negotiated with the seller to have him pay some or all of the points. If so, this would have been specified in the contract.
- ☐ Appraisal fee. This is usually paid by the buyer.
- ☐ Lender's inspection fee. This applies only to new houses and is paid by the buyer.
- ☐ Credit report fee. This is for the credit check on you done by the lender. It is usually paid at the closing, but the lender might require payment at the time of the mortgage application.
- ☐ Recording fees.
- ☐ Taxes. While these will normally be included as part of your mortgage payment, you might be asked to prepay a month, quarter, or more of the taxes at the closing. Taxes owed by the seller might also be paid (someone else writing a check!).
- ☐ Interest due. Lenders leave no stone unturned. You will probably be required to pay the interest on the mortgage due for the few days until your first mortgage payment is due.

Once all the checks have been written, the deed, mortgage, and all inspection and occupancy certificates are issued to you. You are then given the keys to the house. All your hard work and patience has paid off, and you are now a home owner. Pop the champagne and get your real estate agent to take you to lunch. Put away your admittedly thinner checkbook, and start planning what colors you want to paint the bedrooms.

Next time it will be easier!

Real life, real answers.

The up-to-date library of personal financial information

How to make basic investment decisions
by Neal Ochsner

Planning for a financially secure retirement
by Jim Jenks and Brian Zevnik

How to borrow money and use credit
by Martin Weiss

How to pay for your child's college education
by Chuck Lawliss and Barry McCarty

Your will and estate planning
by Fred Tillman and Susan G. Parker

How to protect your family with insurance
by Virginia Applegarth

The easy family budget
by Jerald W. Mason

How to buy your first home
by Peter Jones

Planning for long-term health care
by Harold Evensky

Financial planning for the two-career family
by Candace E. Trunzo